First World War
and Army of Occupation
War Diary
France, Belgium and Germany

47 DIVISION
142 Infantry Brigade,
Brigade Machine Gun Company
10 December 1915 - 28 February 1918

WO95/2744/3

The Naval & Military Press Ltd
www.nmarchive.com
Published in association with The National Archives

Published by

The Naval & Military Press Ltd

Unit 10 Ridgewood Industrial Park,

Uckfield, East Sussex,

TN22 5QE England

Tel: +44 (0) 1825 749494

www.naval-military-press.com

www.nmarchive.com

This diary has been reprinted in facsimile from the original. Any imperfections are inevitably reproduced and the quality may fall short of modern type and cartographic standards.

© Crown Copyright
Images reproduced by permission of The National Archives, London, England, 2015.

Contents

Document type	Place/Title	Date From	Date To
Heading	WO95/2744-3 47 Div 142 Inf Bde Brigade M.G.C Dec 15-Feb 18		
Heading	47th Division 142nd Infy Bde 142nd Machine Gun Coy. Dec 1915 Feb 1918		
Heading	142nd Inf. Bde. 47th Division War Diary 142nd Infantry Brigade Machine Gun Company December 1915 (10.12.15-31.12.15)		
War Diary	Allouagne	10/12/1915	14/12/1915
War Diary	Sailly-La-Bourse	15/12/1915	15/12/1915
War Diary	D1 2, Trenches Hqs & Reserve Teams S.la.B	16/12/1915	23/12/1915
War Diary	Sailly-La-Bourse	24/12/1915	26/12/1915
War Diary	Trenches C 1+2 Hqs & Reserve Teams Sailly-La-Bourse	27/12/1915	27/12/1915
War Diary	Noyelles	28/12/1915	31/12/1915
Heading	142 Bde M Gun Coy Jan Vol II		
War Diary	Noyelles & Trenches C. Sector	01/01/1916	03/01/1916
War Diary	Noyelles & Verquin	04/01/1916	04/01/1916
War Diary	Verquin & Houchin	05/01/1916	05/01/1916
War Diary	Houchin	06/01/1916	06/01/1916
War Diary	Houchin & Braquemont	07/01/1916	07/01/1916
War Diary	Braquemont & Maroc Sub-Sections B.C.& D	08/01/1916	08/01/1916
War Diary	Maroc Sub-Sector B.C.& D	09/01/1916	15/01/1916
War Diary	Maroc & Les Brebis	16/01/1916	20/01/1916
War Diary	Les Brebis & Loos	20/01/1916	20/01/1916
War Diary	Loos	21/01/1916	28/01/1916
War Diary	Les Brebis	29/01/1916	31/01/1916
Heading	142 Bde M Gun Coy Feb Vol III		
War Diary	Maroc	01/02/1916	09/02/1916
War Diary	Les Brebis	10/02/1916	14/02/1916
War Diary	Caucy. A. La Tour	15/02/1916	16/02/1916
War Diary	Allouagne	17/02/1916	22/02/1916
War Diary	Rupigny	23/02/1916	29/02/1916
Heading	142 Bde M Gun Coy Vol IV		
War Diary	Allouagne	01/03/1916	06/03/1916
War Diary	Hersin	07/03/1916	15/03/1916
War Diary	Estree Cauchy	16/03/1916	21/03/1916
War Diary	Gouy Servins	21/03/1916	21/03/1916
War Diary	Petit Servins	22/03/1916	31/03/1916
Heading	142 Bde M Gun Coy Vol V		
War Diary	Petit Servins	01/04/1916	30/04/1916
War Diary	Carency Sector	01/05/1916	26/05/1916
War Diary	Petit Servins Divion	27/05/1916	27/05/1916
War Diary	Divion	28/05/1916	10/06/1916
War Diary	Divion And Bouvigny Wood	11/06/1916	13/06/1916
War Diary	Hersin	14/06/1916	30/06/1916
Heading	142nd Brigade 47th Division 142nd Machine Gun Company July 1916		
Miscellaneous	Headquarters 142nd Inf Bde	03/08/1916	03/08/1916
War Diary	Lorette and Hersin	01/07/1916	01/07/1916
War Diary	Lorette Angres and Hersin	02/07/1916	07/07/1916

Type	Description	From	To
War Diary	Lorette and Hersin	08/07/1916	14/07/1916
War Diary	Lorette Souchez Sector and Aix Noulette	15/07/1916	27/07/1916
War Diary	Hersin	28/07/1916	28/07/1916
War Diary	Monneville	28/07/1916	29/07/1916
War Diary	Magnicourt Sur Canche	30/07/1916	31/07/1916
Operation(al) Order(s)	142nd Bde M.G. Coy Operation Order No. 2 Appendix A	16/07/1916	16/07/1916
Operation(al) Order(s)	142nd Inf Bde M.G. Coy Relief Order No. 1	26/07/1916	26/07/1916
Heading	142nd Brigade 47th Division 142nd Brigade Machine Gun Company August 1916		
Miscellaneous	Headquarters 142 Inf Bde	03/09/1916	03/09/1916
War Diary	Magnicourt-Sur-Canche	01/08/1916	01/08/1916
War Diary	Mezerolles	02/08/1916	04/08/1916
War Diary	Maizicourt	05/08/1916	05/08/1916
War Diary	Drugy	05/08/1916	20/08/1916
War Diary	Bellancourt	20/08/1916	20/08/1916
War Diary	Bethencourt	21/08/1916	21/08/1916
War Diary	Villers Bocage	22/08/1916	22/08/1916
War Diary	Lahoussoye	23/08/1916	10/09/1916
War Diary	Bazentin Le Grand and F.I.D	11/09/1916	14/09/1916
War Diary	Fricourt Farm	15/09/1916	15/09/1916
War Diary	Bazentin Le Grand	16/09/1916	20/09/1916
War Diary	Blackwood	21/09/1916	21/09/1916
War Diary	Millencourt	22/09/1916	30/09/1916
War Diary	Mametz Wood	01/10/1916	01/10/1916
War Diary	Bazentin-Le-Grand	02/10/1916	09/10/1916
War Diary	Laiveville	10/10/1916	14/10/1916
War Diary	Longpre Les Corps Sants	15/10/1916	15/10/1916
War Diary	Vauchelles	16/10/1916	16/10/1916
War Diary	L 23	17/10/1916	19/10/1916
War Diary	Ypres	19/10/1916	23/10/1916
War Diary	Hill 60 Sector	23/10/1916	09/11/1916
War Diary	Scottish Line G 23.a.9.6	10/11/1916	18/11/1916
War Diary	Bluff Sector	18/11/1916	30/11/1916
War Diary	Canal Sub Sector	01/12/1916	08/12/1916
War Diary	Scottish Lines	09/12/1916	20/12/1916
War Diary	Railway Subsector	21/12/1916	24/12/1916
War Diary	Railway Dugouts	25/12/1916	25/12/1916
War Diary	Railway Subsector	26/12/1916	31/03/1917
War Diary	Belgium	23/03/1917	31/03/1917
Miscellaneous	Headquarters 142 Inf Bde	02/05/1917	02/05/1917
War Diary	Railway Subsector	01/04/1917	09/04/1917
War Diary	Canal Sub Sector	10/04/1917	30/04/1917
War Diary	Halifax Camp	01/05/1917	01/05/1917
War Diary	Canal Sub Sector	02/05/1917	31/05/1917
Operation(al) Order(s)	C Machine Gun Company Relief Orders No. 1 By Major E.E. Spencer Cmdg.		
Operation(al) Order(s)	C Machine Gun Company Relief Orders No. 2 By Major E.E. Spencer Cmdg.	17/05/1917	17/05/1917
Operation(al) Order(s)	C Machine Gun Company Relief Order No. 3 By Major E.E. Spencer Cmdg.	28/05/1917	28/05/1917
Miscellaneous	142 M.G. Coy Instructions In Accordance With Second Army Offensive Scheme	26/05/1917	26/05/1917
Miscellaneous	Times Of Advance Of Infantry		
Miscellaneous	142 M.G. Coy Instructions In Accordance With Second Army Offensive Scheme	27/05/1917	27/05/1917

Type	Description	From	To
War Diary	Canal Sub Sector	01/06/1917	10/06/1917
War Diary	Canal Sub Sector & Ouderdom	11/06/1917	11/06/1917
War Diary	Canal Subsector & Heksken	12/06/1917	12/06/1917
War Diary	Canal Sub Sector & Caestre	13/06/1917	14/06/1917
War Diary	Canal Subsector & Racquinghem	14/06/1917	14/06/1917
War Diary	Racquinghem & Heksken	15/06/1917	15/06/1917
War Diary	Racquinghem & Silvestre St Cappel	16/06/1917	16/06/1917
War Diary	Racquinghem	17/06/1917	30/06/1917
Operation(al) Order(s)	C Machine Gun Company Relief Order No. 4 By Major E.E. Spencer Cmdg.	02/06/1917	02/06/1917
Miscellaneous	Report On The Part Taken By The 142 M.G.Coy The Operations In The Canal Sub Sector	10/06/1917	10/06/1917
Map	Map A		
Operation(al) Order(s)	C Machine Gun Company Move Order No. 5 By Major E.E. Spencer Cmdg.	26/06/1917	26/06/1917
Miscellaneous	Amendment To "C" Machine Gun Company Move Order No. 5 By Major E.E. Spencer Cmdg	26/06/1917	26/06/1917
Miscellaneous	C Machine Gun Coy Move Orders By Major E.E. Spencer Comdg	27/06/1917	27/06/1917
Operation(al) Order(s)	C Machine Gun Company Relief Order No. 6 By Major E.E. Spencer Cmdg.	29/06/1917	29/06/1917
War Diary	Dammstrasse	01/07/1917	10/07/1917
War Diary	Murrumbidgee Camp La Ctytte	11/07/1917	22/07/1917
War Diary	Chippewa Camp	23/07/1917	30/07/1917
War Diary	Caterpillar Crater	31/07/1917	31/07/1917
Operation(al) Order(s)	C Machine Gun Company Relief Order No. 8 By Capt. C.G. Davies Cmdg.	08/07/1917	08/07/1917
Operation(al) Order(s)	C Machine Gun Company Relief Order No. 9 By Major E.E. Spencer Cmdg.	15/07/1917	15/07/1917
Operation(al) Order(s)	C Machine Gun Company Operation Order No. 10 By Capt. C.G. Davies Cmdg.	25/07/1917	25/07/1917
War Diary	Bluff Sector Ypres	01/08/1917	31/08/1917
Miscellaneous	Guns & Equipment will Proceed to the forward area by Limber Under Arrangements		
Miscellaneous	Ref Attached Copy Of 41st Div Order No. 149	04/08/1917	04/08/1917
Operation(al) Order(s)	Copy Of 41st Division Order No. 149	04/08/1917	04/08/1917
War Diary		01/09/1917	31/10/1917
Miscellaneous	142 Inf Bde	02/12/1917	02/12/1917
War Diary	Gavrelle Sector	01/11/1917	31/12/1917
Miscellaneous	Report On Action Of "B" Section	07/12/1917	07/12/1917
War Diary		01/01/1918	08/01/1918
War Diary	Flesquieres Right Sub Sector	09/01/1918	13/01/1918
War Diary	Bertincourt	14/01/1918	18/01/1918
War Diary	Flesquieres Left Sub Sector	19/01/1918	31/01/1918
War Diary	In The Field	01/02/1918	28/02/1918

WO95/2744 (3)

47 Div   142 Inf Bde

Brigade M.G.C.

Dec '15 – Feb '18

47TH DIVISION
142ND INFY BDE

142ND MACHINE GUN COY.
DEC 1915-FEB 1918

142nd Inf. Bde.
47th Division.

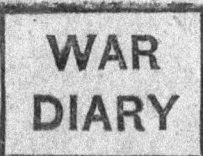

142nd Infantry Brigade Machine Gun Company.

DECEMBER

1915

(10.12.15-31.12.15)

Secret.

I

Army Form C. 2118.

WAR DIARY
or
INTELLIGENCE SUMMARY.

142nd Inf Brigade. Machine Gun Company
10 Dec. 1915 - 31 Dec. 1915

(Erase heading not required.)

Instructions regarding War Diaries and Intelligence Summaries are contained in F.S. Regs., Part II. and the Staff Manual respectively. Title pages will be prepared in manuscript.

Hour, Date, Place		Summary of Events and Information	Remarks and references to Appendices
Dec. 10. 1915	ALLOUAGNE	Machine Gun Company becomes a separate unit 47th Division in Corps reserve. Weather mild and changeable.	EW
11th	do	ditt. Company undergoing training & instruction	
12th	do	ditt. " " " "	
13th	do	Very fine " " " "	
14th	do	Fine. The Company left ALLOUAGNE at 8.0 A.M. and proceeded to SAILLY-LA-BOURSE entraining at LILLERS and detraining at NOEUX-LES-MINES. Thence by road. Billets were occupied L.3 & SAILLY-ANNEQUIN road.	EW
15th	SAILLY-LA-BOURSE.	Weather fair, inclined rain. Five guns proceeded to "D" Section, one was placed in D.1. front line remaining four relieved 2.2nd Bn. Loewes guns in near positions. The Company changed from present billets to billets siting in L.3.a	EW
16th	D.1.&2. Trenches Hqs. & reserve teams S. La B.	ditt. Work commenced on emplacements. Enemy's Artillery not unusually active.	EW

Secret

Army Form C. 2118.

WAR DIARY
or
INTELLIGENCE SUMMARY. 1 & 2 Inf. Brigade Machine Gun Coy
(Erase heading not required.)

Dec 10. 1915 – Dec 31st 1915

Instructions regarding War Diaries and Intelligence Summaries are contained in F.S.Regs., Part II. and the Staff Manual respectively. Title pages will be prepared in manuscript.

Hour, Date, Place			Summary of Events and Information	Remarks and references to Appendices
Dec. 17th	Trenches D1+2 Hq. + reserve teams Sailly – La Bourse	W/st.	Gun teams in trenches changed, and two more guns sent to line. Enemy's artillery again active and their machine guns fired on our reserve trenches intermittently during the hours of darkness. Our machine guns fired on cross roads & in rear of enemy's lines.	
18th	do. do.	Weather changeable. Usual amount of artillery + rifle fire took place		
19th	do. do.	Fine.	Gun teams relieved. Nothing unusual occurred	
10.30 A.M. 20th	do. do.	Fine.	Preparations made to fire in conjunction with artillery bombardment on enemy's front line. Bombardment postponed owing to mist prevailing at the time.	
21st	do. do.	Fair.	Gun teams relieved. The 2nd Division on our left made a gas attack commencing at 8 h.m. The enemy replied by a heavy bombardment on our front and reserve lines. No casualties occurred in the Coy. but one gun was slightly damaged, a piece of shell fracturing travel casing	

B. B. Jones Lieut
OC 1st & 2nd Inf. Bde. M.G. Coy

Secret

Army Form C. 2118.

WAR DIARY
or
INTELLIGENCE SUMMARY.

142nd Inf. Brigade Machine Gun Coy

(Erase heading not required.)

Dec 10th 1915 – Dec 31st 1915

Instructions regarding War Diaries and Intelligence Summaries are contained in F.S. Regs., Part II. and the Staff Manual respectively. Title pages will be prepared in manuscript.

Hour, Date, Place	Summary of Events and Information	Remarks and references to Appendices
9 a.m. Dec. 22nd 1915. D 1+2 Trenches Hqs + Reserve teams in S.L.B.	Weather wet. O.C. B M.G Coy 141st Inf Brigade inspected emplacements preparatory to relieving this day. Enemy artillery continued to do nothing. Our guns continued to employ overhead fire at night. Enemy did not attempt to shell emplacements. 3rd Hamps Batt. Regt. machine gun Sectn. temporarily attached for duty.	Seen ex Lieut Col J. [signature] OC 142nd Bde M.G.
5.00 a.m. Dec 23rd 1915 D 1+2 Trenches Hqs + Reserve teams in S.L.B.	Weather fine. Guides were sent to VERMELLES Church to conduct relieving unit to emplacements. Relief completed at 6.30 a.m. and relieved teams reached billets at 10.0 a.m.	
Dec 24th 1915 SAILLY-LA-BOURSE	Rainy. 142nd Infantry Brigade in Divisional Reserve. Interior economy.	
9.30 a.m. Dec. 25th 1915 do.	Wet. Church parade held in Divisional Recreation Room L.3.a.9.5.	
10.30 a.m. Dec 26th 1915 do.	Wet. Representative unit guide of 140th Inf. Brigade machine gun Coy. and was shown out emplacements in C section & guns left SAILLY-LA-BOURSE at 7 p.m. to relieve 140th Inf Brigade in C section, guns of which were placed in front line, the remaining four lined up position for overhead fire in D.B.1st

Secret

Army Form C. 2118.

WAR DIARY
or
INTELLIGENCE SUMMARY.
(Erase heading not required.)

142nd Inf. Brigade Machine Gun Coy.

10 Dec. 1915 - 31st Dec. 1915

E.E. Spencer / Lieut
O.C. 142nd Inf Bde M.G. Coy.

Hour, Date, Place	Summary of Events and Information	Remarks and references to Appendices
7.0 a.m. 27 Dec. 1915 Trenches C 1+2 Hq. + reserve teams SAILLY-LA-BOURSE	Hq. + Reserve teams left SAILLY-LA-BOURSE and took over the billets of the 140th Inf. Brigade at NOYELLES. There was a certain amount of shelling, but C section in general was fairly quiet. Our rear guns fired during the night on the DUMP on our left, and at the trenches in its vicinity. 1st Division on our right. 141st Inf. Brigade on our left.	
28 Dec. 1915 C 1+2 NOYELLES	Faint but strong wind. Gun teams were relieved at 4 p.m. The enemy shelled NOYELLES slightly between 10.0 a.m. & 11.0 a.m., but no damage was done. The line was exceptionally quiet.	
29 Dec. 1915 do. do.	Faint. C 2 was slightly shelled in the morning, mostly on front line + O.B.1. Throughout night enemy heavy shelling (supposed 59 howitzer) fell on the support lines near left leg of HAIRPIN and on STANSFIELD ROAD + near trench at roughly 12 mm. labrune. Our rear guns again fired on Langille named above.	
7.0 a.m. 30 Dec. 1915 do. do.	Wet. The enemy heavily shelled our front line trenches, mainly on the dug-out of gun team just left of left leg of HAIRPIN. Casualties - gun team shelled two wounded. The enemy's artillery again shelled our front + reserve lines during the afternoon. Contd.	

Secret.

Army Form C. 2118.

1st & 2nd Inf. Brigade Machine Gun Coy.

10 Dec. 1915 – 31st Dec. 1915

WAR DIARY
OR
INTELLIGENCE SUMMARY.
(*Erase heading not required.*)

Instructions regarding War Diaries and Intelligence Summaries are contained in F.S. Regs., Part II. and the Staff Manual respectively. Title pages will be prepared in manuscript.

Hour, Date, Place	Summary of Events and Information	Remarks and references to Appendices
4.15 p.m. 30 Dec. 1915 C 1+2 NOYELLES (contd)	Enemy exploded several mines at the top of HAIRPIN. Three left front guns immediately opened fire on crater with probably good effect. One gun on left of O.B.1 opened long range fire in direction of HAIRPIN. On the mines during captured the enemy immediately opened heavy artillery fire on our front line and communication trenches. No guns were injured but two reliefs proceeding to their places were caught in the enemy barrage of fire and the following casualties resulted, one killed and eight wounded. A further supply of ammunition was immediately sent up, also two extra guns, and remainder of Coy stood to. The enemy however did not attack.	
31 Dec. 1915 do. do.	We experienced a certain amount of shelling especially near GOEBEN ALLEY during the day. Our front guns fired on the enemy's front line wire to impede any work that the enemy may have been engaged on there.	

B.Louw Smith
OC 1st & 2nd Inf/Bde. M.G. Coy

44

14 & 2 Bde M Gun Coy

Jan
Vol II

47

"142nd Infantry Bde. Machine Gun Coy.

WAR DIARY
or
INTELLIGENCE SUMMARY.
(Erase heading not required.)

Army Form C. 2118.

January 1916

Hour, Date, Place	Summary of Events and Information	Remarks and references to Appendices
January 1st 1916	Very windy & wet. Enemy unusually quiet.	Map references for Coy. H.Q. on which there were no Coy. guns in line taken from 36B (1/10000). Other references from French map (1/20000).
2nd	Windy & wet. A little shelling on left of Sector. Enemy fired on (i) South Side of DUMP (ii) Track running NE from CRATER (iii) CRATER on HAIRPIN. Two guns relieved by Cavalry Brigade.	
3rd	Fine. Enemy quiet. Four guns relieved by Cavalry Brigade.	
NOYELLES→VERQUIN 4th	Fine. Coy left NOYELLES for VERQUIN at 6.30 a.m. H.Q.E.29.d.5.9	Divisional Reserve.
VERQUIN→HOUCHIN 5th	Fine. Coy left VERQUIN for HOUCHIN at 3.30 p.m. H.Q.K.15.a.29	— " —
HOUCHIN 6th	Dull. Four guns sent to Divisional school.	— " —
HOUCHIN→BRAQUEMONT 7th	Wet. Coy left HOUCHIN for BRAQUEMONT at 2 p.m. Coy representative reconnoitred new line to be taken over by Coy. H.Q. L.19.c.5.10.	— " —
BRAQUEMONT→MAROC 8th Sub Section BC+D	Fair. Coy left BRAQUEMONT for MAROC at 12 noon. The Coy relieved 140th Inf. Bde. M.G. Coy in MAROC Sector at 1.30 p.m. Coy H.Q. in SOUTH MAROC M2d 4½.5. On our right French troops. On our left 141st Inf. Bde. Four guns returned from Divisional School.	
MAROC 9th	Fine. Heavy shelling during the afternoon.	

142nd Inf. Bde. Machine Gun Coy.

Army Form C. 2118.

WAR DIARY
or
INTELLIGENCE SUMMARY.
(Erase heading not required.)

January 1916

Instructions regarding War Diaries and Intelligence Summaries are contained in F.S. Regs., Part II and the Staff Manual respectively. Title pages will be prepared in manuscript.

Hour, Date, Place	Summary of Events and Information	Remarks and references to Appendices
MAROC Subsection B,C,&D Jany 10th 1916	Fine. Billets shelled during the day.	
MAROC — do — 11th	Fair. Artillery active during the day on Billets and Communication Trenches	
MAROC — do — 12th	Fine. Some shelling during the day. Troops on our left relieved by 140th Inf. Bde.	
MAROC — do — 13th	Fine. Usual artillery activity during the day	
MAROC — do — 14th	— do — — do — — do —	
MAROC — do — 15th	— do — — do — — do —	
MAROC & LES BREBIS 16th	Dull. Slight shelling. Relieved at 1:30 p.m. by 141st Inf. Bde. left MAROC for LES BREBIS. HQ L.35.b.4.4.	
LES BREBIS 17th	Dull. Coy in Divisional Reserve. Shower becoming	
LES BREBIS 18th	Dull + showery. Billets shelled slightly	
LES BREBIS 19th	Fine. Line to be occupied by Coy reconnoitred at 9:30 a.m. by representatives. LES BREBIS shelled slightly.	
LES BREBIS & LOOS 20th	Showery. Coy left LES BREBIS at 12:30 p.m. and relieved 140th Inf Bde M.G. Co. in LOOS sector. HQ G.35.b.1.1. On our right 141st Inf. Bde. on our left 15th Division	

Army Form C. 2118

142nd Inf. Bde Machine Gun Cy

WAR DIARY
or
INTELLIGENCE SUMMARY

(Erase heading not required.)

Instructions regarding War Diaries and Intelligence Summaries are contained in F.S. Regs., Part II. and the Staff Manual respectively. Title Pages will be prepared in manuscript.

Place	Date	Hour	Summary of Events and Information	Remarks and references to Appendices
LOOS	21/1/16	10.30pm	Dull. Some artillery activity during day.	
		10.30pm	Bombers on both sides were active along our front, especially in the vicinity of SNIPERS HOUSE M6c19	
LOOS	22/1/16		Dull. Artillery not unusually active. Very clear moonlight night.	
LOOS	23/1/16	2 a.m	R.E.'s fired a mine at M.5.b.9.1. Our artillery immediately opened fire, and two of the Company machine guns swept the ground between the newly formed Crater and the enemy front line with a view to converging working party in the Crater. About 2,000 rounds were fired by those machine guns. The enemy reply was very late, fifteen minutes elapsed between the firing of the mine and the enemy artillery opening fire. Things became normal.	
		3.30 a.m	During the morning artillery was unusually quiet but there was considerable activity between 2.30 pm and 3.30 p.m. During the night the enemy sent a quantity of rifle grenades and trench mortar bombs in the vicinity of the COPSE and Crater	
LOOS	24/1/16		Dull. Enemy shelled our communication trenches and LOOS intermittently during the day. Trim teams were changed round from front to rear for relief purposes. Night fairly quiet, except for considerable sniping.	

1 & 2nd Gnj. Bde Machine Gun Coy

WAR DIARY or INTELLIGENCE SUMMARY

Army Form C. 2118

(Erase heading not required.)

Place	Date	Hour	Summary of Events and Information	Remarks and references to Appendices
LOOS	25/1/16		Fine. Usual artillery activity during day, and during the night the enemy were active with rifle grenades in the neighbourhood of the PYLONS, CRASSIER and the COPSE.	Bones/Kent
		11.30 pm ?	Single shots were fired on some mules CITÉ St PIERRE from G 35 d. 5 5 b and along the LENS - BETHUNE road from G 35 c 5 b. One casualty in police two 8.0 a.m.	
LOOS	26/1/16		Weather fine in the morning, inclined to rain later. Reserve trenches, communication trenches and LOOS were shelled very heavily during the greater part of the day. Gas shells were smelt during this bombardment, but none exploded in our neighbourhood. The enemy again shelled our reserve trenches with shrapnel between 10.30 p.m. and midnight causing several casualties to working parties. Our new guns did not fire during the night to avoid annoying the numerous parties in front of them.	
LOOS	27/1/16	10.0 am	Weather fine. The enemy again shelled front, reserve lines and communication trenches during the greater part of the day. Considerable damage being done to the trenches leading to the COPSE. One shell landing on machine gun dug-out at M 6. a. 7. 0. wounded three of the team, the gun and emplacement escaping.	
LOOS	28/1/16	6 a.m.	Weather fine. Emplacement at M 6. a. 6. 1. struck by rifle grenade, two men sustaining injury, one fatal.	P.T.O.

Army Form C. 2118

1st 2nd Gnfi. Bde. Machine Gun Coy.

WAR DIARY
or
INTELLIGENCE SUMMARY
(Erase heading not required.)

Place	Date	Hour	Summary of Events and Information	Remarks and references to Appendices
LOOS	28/1/16	10 p.m.	Guides met incoming Company at MINE GATES, MAROC.	
		11.15 p.m.	Numbers reported having reached the barricade HIGH STREET, LOOS, and guide leading guns to their position.	
LES BREBIS	29/1/16	2.50 a.m.	Last gun reported on limbers and remainder of company moving off.	
		2.30 a.m.	Relief complete, units 142nd Gnfi. Bde.	
		4.30 a.m.	Company billeted in LES BREBIS.	
		10.0 a.m.	Weather fine. Interior economy.	
		2.30 p.m.		
LES BREBIS	30/1/16		Weather fine. Interior economy. Four positions reconnoitered at G.34.d. for occupation in the event of an alarm.	
LES BREBIS	31/1/16	7.45 p.m.	Weather fine. Interior economy. Intense bombardment on the German lines took place, lasting approximately twenty minutes. No reply from the enemy artillery on LES BREBIS.	8/2/1916 Derwent Lieut.

HGreenhead
O.C. Bde. M.G. Coy

47

14 2 Bde M Gun Coy
Feb
Vol III

Army Form C. 2118

WAR DIARY
or
INTELLIGENCE SUMMARY
(Erase heading not required.)

142nd Infantry Brigade Machine Gun Company   1/2/16 to 29/2/16

Instructions regarding War Diaries and Intelligence Summaries are contained in F.S. Regs., Part II. and the Staff Manual respectively. Title Pages will be prepared in manuscript.

Place	Date	Hour	Summary of Events and Information	Remarks and references to Appendices
Maroc	1/2/16	12.30 PM	Bombs dropped on Les Brebis by German Aeroplane.	
		10.30 "	The Company relieved 140th Bgd Machine Gun Company in Maroc Sect. 8 Guns are in Front Line. 4 Guns in North Maroc and it in South Maroc. Weather fine.	
Maroc	2/2/16		Moved one Gun from No 3 emplacement to No 5. Very slight shelling. Weather fine.	
Maroc	3/2/16		Some shelling in afternoon, evening quiet. Weather fine.	
Maroc	4/2/16		Slight shelling during afternoon. During the night the enemy was heard working in the trenches at M9 D49. New positions reconnoitred in EMBANKMENT. Weather wet and windy.	
Maroc	5/2/16		Relief took place. Two Guns were fired from our support line. From temporary positions, bursts of 30 rounds, on objects being the church at St Pierre. Guns afterwards replaced in previous positions. Very slight shelling in afternoon. Weather windy. Bright.	

WAR DIARY
or
INTELLIGENCE SUMMARY

Army Form C. 2118

142nd Inf. Brigade Machine Gun Company. 1/7/16 to 29/7/16

(Erase heading not required.)

Place	Date	Hour	Summary of Events and Information	Remarks and references to Appendices
Maroc	6/7/16		Enemy working at M.9 D.6.8. Enemy slightly shelled left section of our front line. We Trench fire Company for duty. Weather Dull.	
Maroc	7/7/16		Enemy working party active on left of Sectn, work continued in front M.9 D.6.1. Enemy shelled MIDDLE ALLEY. slightly during the morning. Emplacement at M+C 6.10 finished. 2nd Lorn-on were relieved and proceeded to rejoin their unit. Weather Dull and Windy	
Maroc	8/7/16		Enemy working during the night at M10 C 47k. This front was fired upon. Gun mounted in new position at M+C 6 .10.	
Maroc	9/7/16	10.30 PM	The Company was relieved by 141st Brigade. Proceeded to Les Brebis and Billeted there.	
		11 AM	Enemy Aeroplane dropped 4 Bombs on our lines, which did not explode.	
		4 AM	A Mine was exploded by us in Rort. Sectn. Very little reply by enemy Artillery. Series of explosions in Enemys lines in M.10.6. Weather fine and cool	

WAR DIARY
or
INTELLIGENCE SUMMARY

Army Form C. 2118

142nd Infantry Brigade Machine Gun Company. 10/2/16 to 78/2/16

Place	Date	Hour	Summary of Events and Information	Remarks and references to Appendices
Sailly Labourse	10/2/16	4.30 P.M	1 Section of 4 Guns, under Lt Shally sent to Loos Sector, under command of C.O. 4th Batt. Royal Welsh Fusiliers. Weather fine. Gun and limber cleaning during the morning. Weather fine.	
"	11/2/16			
"	12/2/16		Weather fair. °Interior Economy.	
"	13/2/16		Weather fair. Orders received to stand by for practice Gas attack.	
"	14/2/16		The Company was relieved by 3rd Brigade Machine Gun Coy who took over our Billets. The company proceeded to Rème for Mauro and entrained. Detrained at LILLERS and marched to CAUCHY. a. LA. TOUR and billetted there. Weather wet and Windy.	
CAUCY. A. LA TOUR	15/2/16	10 AM	Feet inspection. Weather fine during morning. Rain during the afternoon.	
"	16/2/16	6.30 AM	The company proceeded to ALLOUAGNE and Billetted there. Weather very wet and Windy	JP-

WAR DIARY
or
INTELLIGENCE SUMMARY

142nd Infantry Bde. Machine Gun Coy.

Army Form C. 2118

Place	Date	Hour	Summary of Events and Information	Remarks and references to Appendices
ABBEVILLE	17/9/16	—	Rifle and Bayonet inspection, followed by Run and gun cleaning. Weather fair.	
"	18/9/16	—	Interior Economy. Weather fair.	
"	19/9/16	—	Interior Economy. Weather Dull.	
"	20/9/16	—	Interior Economy. Weather fine.	
"	21/9/16	—	Programme of work begun. Vickers Gun classes formed, but disbanded owing to Brigade movement.	
"	22/9/16	—	The Company marched to RUPIGNY. A. BOMY and BUILLER there. Weather very cold and heavy snowfall.	
RUPIGNY	23/9/16	—	Weather too bad for tactical exercise. Heavy fall of snow.	
"	24/9/16	—	Weather fine. Heavy fall of snow. The company engaged in tactical exercises morning and afternoon.	

Army Form C. 2118

WAR DIARY
or
INTELLIGENCE SUMMARY
(Erase heading not required.)

142nd Inf. Brigade Machine Gun Coy.

Instructions regarding War Diaries and Intelligence Summaries are contained in F. S. Regs., Part II. and the Staff Manual respectively. Title Pages will be prepared in manuscript.

Place	Date	Hour	Summary of Events and Information	Remarks and references to Appendices
RUPIGNY	25/2/16		Weather very bad. Heavy fall of snow. The company took part in Brigade Tactical exercise.	
"	26/2/16		Weather very bad. Cold and snow. Lecture given to Company in Billets.	
"	27/2/16	12 noon	Weather bad. Some signs of a thaw. The Company proceeded to take part in Brigade Tactical Exercise but operations were cancelled. The company went for a short route march.	
"	28/2/16	9 A.M.	The company proceeded to take part in Brigade Tactical Exercise, but operations were cancelled. Weather cold.	
"	29/2/16	6.30 P.M.	The Company marched to ALLOUAGNE, arrived there at 11.30 P.M. and took over the Billets. Weather Dull.	

1875 Wt. W593/826 1,000,000 4/15 J.B.C. & A. A.D.S.S./Forms/C. 2118.

142   4"

142 Bde M Gun
Coy

Vol IV

WAR DIARY
or
INTELLIGENCE SUMMARY

(Erase heading not required.)

Army Form C. 2118

Place	Date	Hour	Summary of Events and Information	Remarks and references to Appendices
ALLOUAGNE	1/3/16		Company Training. Range practice carried out	
"	2/3/16		Company Training.	
"	3/3/16		Company Training	
"	4/3/16		Company Training } Refresher Course	
"	5/3/16		Church Parade	
"	6/3/16		Company Training	
	7/3/16		Company moved at 8.30 am. to HERSIN. Arrived at 2.30 pm. and was placed at disposal of G.O.C. 2nd Division	
HERSIN	8/3/16		Area taken over from the FRENCH cleared	
"	9/3/16		Company Training	
"	10/3/16		Company Training } Refresher Course	
"	11/3/16		Company Training	
"	12/3/16		Company Training. Two support line reconnoitred under 2nd. Division Arrangements and gun emplacements sited	
"	13/3/16		Company Training. Working party supplied to work on emplacements previously sited	
"	14/3/16		Company Training. do do do.	

Army Form C. 2118

WAR DIARY or INTELLIGENCE SUMMARY

(Erase heading not required.)

Instructions regarding War Diaries and Intelligence Summaries are contained in F. S. Regs., Part II. and the Staff Manual respectively. Title Pages will be prepared in manuscript.

Place	Date	Hour	Summary of Events and Information	Remarks and references to Appendices
HERSIN	15/3/16		Company Training. Working party supplied to work on emplacements previously cited	
ESTRÉE CAUCHY	16/3/16		Company left for ESTRÉE CAUCHY at 9.30 a.m. Arrived 11.30 a.m. and Coys were billeted vacated by 12th D.L.I.	
"	17/3/16		Company Training & Refresher Course.	
"	18/3/16		Company Training	
"	19/3/16		Transport & Gun Stores moved at 4 p.m. to PETIT SERVINS	
"	20/3/16		One Section (4 guns) moved at 9 a.m. to BOUVIGNY HUTS and came under orders of C.O. 9th Bn. Lon. Reg.	
"	21/3/16		One Section ( ) relieved section in BOUVIGNY HUTS the latter section moving to LORETTE Trenches	
GUOY SERVINS			Remainder of Company moved at 4.30 p.m. to GUOY SERVINS and was billeted	
PETIT SERVINS	22/3/16		The two sections in GUOY SERVINS moved at 11.30 a.m. to PETIT SERVINS and were billeted	
"	23/3/16		Sections in which employed in cleaning Area.	
"	24/3/16		do.	
"	25/3/16		Company Training	
"	26/3/16		One Section from PETIT SERVINS moved off at 6 p.m. and relieved one section in 9th B.M.G. Coy in LEFT SUBSECTOR. Section in LORETTE Trenches was relieved by section of 141st B.M.G. Coy and proceeded to relieve one section 141st B.M.G. Coy in ABLAIN ST NAZARE Section in BOUVIGNY HUTS relieved by one section 141st Bde. Coy and returned to PETIT SERVINS	R.P.Vernor Capt.

Army Form C. 2118

WAR DIARY
or
INTELLIGENCE SUMMARY
(Erase heading not required.)

Instructions regarding War Diaries and Intelligence Summaries are contained in F. S. Regs., Part II. and the Staff Manual respectively. Title Pages will be prepared in manuscript.

Place	Date	Hour	Summary of Events and Information	Remarks and references to Appendices
PETIT SERWINS	27/3/16		Two Sections from PETIT SERWINS relieved two Sections of 146th Bn P. Coy in CABARET ROUGE and RIGHT SUBSECTOR respectively.	
	28/3/16		Enemy shelled N.E. edge of QUARRY with L.H.V. shells. A new gun position was reconnoitred and communication on the right of left subsector improved.	
	29/3/16		Right and Centre front line emplacements improved. Alternative emplacements commenced. Trenches in vicinity of left front guns improved. Positions reconnoitred on Western slope ZOUAVE Valley.	
	30/3/16		Enemy shelled QUARRY slightly. CABARET ROUGE slightly shelled. One machine Gun's fired on enemy Aeroplane over quarry in the morning. Positions in QUARRY and CABARET ROUGE worked on.	
	31/3/16		Enemy shelled left sector during afternoon, and CABARET ROUGE considerably during the day. CABARET ROUGE - SOUCHEZ was shelled about 8.30 p.m. Several casualties resulting. Emplacements along the front worked on and improved.	

404

142 Bde M Gun Coy

Vol V

WAR DIARY or INTELLIGENCE SUMMARY

(Erase heading not required.)

Army Form C. 2118

Place	Date	Hour	Summary of Events and Information	Remarks and references to Appendices
PETIT SERVINS	1/4/16		Some shelling of left sector during the afternoon. Alternative emplacements commenced.	Spencer Cpl.
	2/4/16		Enemy shelled CABARET ROUGE, CARENCY - SOUCHEZ ROAD with L.H.V. shells from 6.0 p.m. to 8.0 p.m. Positions reconnoitred for the protection of reserve line. Aeroplane was seen to fall from a height of about 4000 feet over LORETTE RIDGE at 3.45 p.m.	
	3/4/16		Company relieved by 141st Infantry Brigade Machine Gun Company.	
	4/4/16		Interior Economy.	
	5/4/16		Company Training. Range practice carried out.	
	6/4/16		Company Training. Range practice carried out.	
	7/4/16		Two sections relieved two sections of 140th Infantry Brigade Machine Gun Company at LORETTE TRENCHES and BOUVIGNY HUTS	
	8/4/16		Alternative emplacements commenced in reserve line.	
	9/4/16		Company take over "B" area. Trench mortar emplacements in left sector deepened and dug out for teams at CABARET ROUGE commenced.	
	10/4/16		Enemy shelled CABARET ROUGE during the afternoon, also the PIMPLE. Emplacements in SWITCH LINE worked on during the night.	
	11/4/16		Enemy shelled CABARET ROUGE between 7.0 and 7.30 p.m. Emplacements worked on in SWITCH and MAISTRE lines.	
	12/4/16		Enemy shelled vicinity of CABARET ROUGE between 9.0 p.m. and 9.0 p.m. Communication trench between emplacements and 130 ROAD deepened and repaired.	
	13/4/16		Enemy shelled ZOUAVE VALLEY very considerably during the latter part of the afternoon, no great damage was done. Trenches and emplacements in left sector worked on.	

Army Form C. 2118

Instructions regarding War Diaries and Intelligence Summaries are contained in F.S. Regs., Part II. and the Staff Manual respectively. Title Pages will be prepared in manuscript.

WAR DIARY
or
INTELLIGENCE SUMMARY
(Erase heading not required.)

Place	Date	Hour	Summary of Events and Information	Remarks and references to Appendices
PETIT SERINS	14/4/16		Fought bombing by the enemy in right PICQUET. Entanglement intact. Rear gun position with at S.6.a.5.9.	Officers Copy
	15/4/16		Some shelling of our front and support lines in left sector. Communication guns worked on.	
	16/4/16		Heavy trench mortaring of our front line. Work continued on.	
	17/4/16		Enemy machine gun fired on CABARET ROUGE road between 8.45 p.m and 15.30 p.m with some success. Emplacement built on RIVER ALLEY 8.8.a.9.9.	
	18/4/16		Enemy machine gun fired on CABARET ROUGE road at 12.30 a.m. Ammunition recess in RIVER ALLEY gun emplacement.	
	19/4/16		Enemy shelled QUARRIES with L.H.V. shell between 5.30 p.m and 6.0 p.m. Iterates very well. Trenches drained.	
	20/4/16		Enemy machine gun fired frequent bursts on CABARET ROUGE road from 9.30 p.m until midnight from the direction of the PIMPLE. Entanglement intact. Tunnel under CABARET ROUGE road tamped out. Pits for screened emplacements on TOPART RIDGE worked on.	
	21/4/16		Enemy shelled left PICQUET during the afternoon. Alternative positions for RIVER ALLEY guns started.	
	22/4/16		Enemy shelled left PICQUET and communication trench to QUARRY with L.H.V. shell between 4.0 p.m and 6.0 p.m. Our machine guns fired on trenches and tracks behind enemy lines.	
	23/4/16		Considerable bombing and trench mortaring in Centre Sector.	
	24/4/16		Entanglement work carried out. Emplacements and trenches in the vicinity of CABARET ROUGE improved.	

Army Form C. 2118

WAR DIARY
or
INTELLIGENCE SUMMARY

(Erase heading not required.)

Instructions regarding War Diaries and Intelligence Summaries are contained in F.S. Regs., Part II. and the Staff Manual respectively. Title Pages will be prepared in manuscript.

Place	Date	Hour	Summary of Events and Information	Remarks and references to Appendices
PETIT SERVINS	27/4/16		Enemy artillery very active during early hours of the morning in the neighbourhood of CABARET ROUGE and CARENCY. Emplacement and trenches in reserve line improved.	[signature]
	28/4/16		Enemy exploded a mine at 9.6.d.9.1. (approx) at 7.0 p.m. Emplacements in QUARRIES worked on and communication improved between CABARET ROUGE & guns. Work continued on SWITCH and MAISTRE junction.	
	29/4/16		Enemy trench mortars very active on "B" subsector during the morning. Discipline improved. Work continued on SWITCH and MAISTRE lines. QUARRY and Lt Piquet positions. Weather exceptionally fine. Enemy's artillery not unusually active, very little sniping during the night. Work was continued on emplacements in the rear lines of defence.	
	30/4/16		Weather fine. Enemy shelled ZOUAVE VALLEY rather heavily during the morning. At 6.51 p.m. enemy exploded a mine of unit SOUTH of the PIMPLE, blowing up part of our front line, a number of casualties among the infantry, but none of this unit. My return gun was ordered without delay to meet the new trench situation, but the enemy did not attempt to attack or take the crater. The rest of the night was unusually quiet.	

[signature] Capt.
O.C. No. 4 Coy
142nd Infantry Brigade

WAR DIARY or INTELLIGENCE SUMMARY

Army Form C. 2118

142 Bde M.G. Coy Vol 6

(Erase heading not required.)

Instructions regarding War Diaries and Intelligence Summaries are contained in F. S. Regs., Part II. and the Staff Manual respectively. Title Pages will be prepared in manuscript.

Place	Date	Hour	Summary of Events and Information	Remarks and references to Appendices
CARENCY SECTOR	1/5/16		Three Sections in trenches, one in reserve. Enemy activity normal.	
"	2/5/16		- do - - do -	
"	3/5/16		- do - - do -	
"	4/5/16		- do - - do -	
"	5/5/16		- do - - do -	
"	6/5/16		- do - Enemy machine Guns very active at night.	
"	7/5/16		- do - Enemy activity normal.	
"	8/5/16		- do - - do -	
"	9/5/16		- do - - do -	
"	10/5/16		- do - - do -	
"	11/5/16		- do - - do -	
"	12/5/16		- do - - do -	
"	13/5/16		- do - - do -	
"	14/5/16		- do - - do -	
"	15/5/16		- do - - do -	
"	16/5/16		- do - - do -	
"	17/5/16		- do - - do -	

Army Form C. 2118

WAR DIARY
or
INTELLIGENCE SUMMARY
(Erase heading not required.)

Instructions regarding War Diaries and Intelligence Summaries are contained in F. S. Regs., Part II. and the Staff Manual respectively. Title Pages will be prepared in manuscript.

Place	Date	Hour	Summary of Events and Information	Remarks and references to Appendices
CARENCY SECTOR	18/5/16		Three Sections in trenches, one in reserve. Enemy activity normal.	
"	19/5/16		- do -	
"	20/5/16		- do -	
"	21/5/16		- do - Enemy activity culminated in an intense bombardment followed by an Infantry Attack on left of which moved the right of this Sector. Reserve Section moved from PETIT SERVINS to VILLERS AU BOIS.	
"	22/5/16		Artillery indulged in reprisal bombardment. Reserve Section stood by at VILLERS AU BOIS.	
"	23/5/16		Reserve Section moved to trenches at CABARET ROUGE. All Sections stood to during assault by our Infantry.	
"	24/5/16		Four Sections in trenches. Considerable artillery activity on both sides. One Section withdrawn at night to PETIT SERVINS.	
"	25/5/16		Conditions normal except that artillery continued very active.	
"	26/5/16		- do - . During the night 26/27 the Company was relieved by 6th Bde. M.G. Coy. and collected at PETIT SERVINS.	
PETIT SERVINS	27/5/16		Company left PETIT SERVINS at 2.30 pm and marched to DIVION arriving at 6.30 pm.	
DIVION	28/5/16		Church Parade. Inspection by G.O.C. 1st Army.	
"	29/5/16		Interior Economy.	
"	30/5/16		Refresher Course started.	
"	31/5/16		Refresher Course continued.	

1875 Wt. W593/826 1,000,000 4/15 J.B.C. & A. A.D.S.S./Forms/C. 2118.

WAR DIARY or INTELLIGENCE SUMMARY

Army Form C. 2118

142 Bde M.G. Coy

Place	Date	Hour	Summary of Events and Information	Remarks and references to Appendices
DIVION	1.6.16		Weather fine. 47th Division in Corps Reserve. Company carried out training in accordance with Programme of Work, comprising technical machine gun work, and open fighting.	Officers
	2.6.16		Weather fine. Company training as above.	
	3.6.16		" " Company training, and lecture, and demonstration on packing limbers	
	4.6.16		" " Church Parade	
	5.6.16	10.0 am	Inspection of whole Company, including Transport by B.G.C. Company training.	
	6.6.16		Company training	
	7.6.16		" "	
	8.6.16		" "	
	9.6.16		" "	
	10.6.16		Slight rain. Range practice	
DIVION and BOUVIGNY WOODS	11.6.16	1.30pm	Nos 1 & 2 Sections moved to BOUVIGNY WOODS, under tactical command of 6th Battn, London Regt, who relieved a Battalion of the 23rd Division. Nos 3 & 4 Sections attended Brigade Church Parade.	
	12.6.16	1.30pm	Nos 1 & 2 Sections took up positions on LORETTE HEIGHTS. Nos 3 & 4 Sections carried out Range Practice and Section training.	
	13.6.16	10.0 am	Headquarters and Nos 3 & 4 Sections moved to HERSIN, and recued with at Q.b.d.1. time of arrival at HERSIN 2.30 pm	
HERSIN	14.6.16		Company occupying LORETTE with two Sections, remaining two Section under tactical command of Reserve Brigade. Division occupying NOULETTE SECTOR	

WAR DIARY or INTELLIGENCE SUMMARY

Army Form C. 2118

(Erase heading not required.)

Place	Date	Hour	Summary of Events and Information	Remarks and references to Appendices
HERSIN	15.6.16		Weather dull. Nos 1 & 2 Sections LORETTE defences, Disposition of guns, front on BATAILLE LINE, two in BOYAU LA PRADE, one in MAISTRE LINE, and one on BATAILLE SWITCH. Remaining two sections carried out section training	
	16.6.16		As above	
	17.6.16		" "	
	18.6.16	6.15 pm	Same. Nos 3 & 4 Sections left HERSIN and carried out relief of remaining two sections	
	19.6.16	3.45 am	Dull. Nos 1 & 2 Sections returned to HERSIN	
		12.0 noon	Pay Parade and cleaning of guns	
	20.6.16		Same. Left half company LORETTE, right half company section training	
	21.6.16		" "	
	22.6.16		" "	
	23.6.16		Changeable "	
	24.6.16		Fast. Entire half company relief	
	25.6.16	6.30 pm	Left half company returned to HERSIN	
	26.6.16	10.0 am	Capt R. BUTLER received MILITARY MEDAL at Brigade Church Parade and Presentation of Diamonds by G.O.C. Division. O.C. Company Sergeants in Command and twelve other ranks attended	
	26.6.16	9.0 am	Changeable. Right half company LORETTE, left half company section training G.O.C. Division made tour of SOUCHEZ SECTOR and LORETTE. New disjointed scheme on LORETTE	
	27.6.16	11.15 pm	Bright. 141st Brigade relieving ANGRES Sub-Sector carried out work on German lines command until not attack successfully.	

141st INF. Bde. M.G. COMPANY
COMMANDING
CAPTAIN
R.J. Isaacs

WAR DIARY or INTELLIGENCE SUMMARY

Army Form C. 2118

Place	Date	Hour	Summary of Events and Information	Remarks and references to Appendices
HERSIN	28.6.16	Weather wet	Right half company LORETTE. Work commenced on new gun positions on BATOILE MINE South of ARRAS ROAD. Left half company drills & lectures. Work on new emplacements continued. Section training	
	29.6.16	fine	" " "	
	30.6.16	dull	" " "	

[Signature]
CAPTAIN
COMMANDING
142nd INF. Bde. M.G. COMPANY

142nd Brigade.
47th Division

142nd MACHINE GUN COMPANY

JULY 1 9 1 6:

Headquarters

142nd Inf Bde

"Confidential"

Herewith War Diary for the month of July 1916.

E Spencer
CAPTAIN
COMMANDING
M.G. COMPANY

3/8/16

Army Form C. 2118

WAR DIARY
or
INTELLIGENCE SUMMARY
(Erase heading not required.)

142 MG Coy

Vol 8

Place	Date	Hour	Summary of Events and Information	Remarks and references to Appendices
LORETTE and HERSIN	1.7.16		Weather fine. Right half Company on LORETTE, left half Company section training.	2/Lt Capt.
		2.30 pm	No 4 Section placed at disposal of 141st Bde. M.G. Coy, and moved to FOSSE 10. 8.30 p.m. No 4 Section relieved a section of 141st Bde M.G. Coy in front system trenches ANGRES Sector.	
LORETTE, ANGRES and HERSIN.	2.7.16		Weather wet. Nos. 1 & 2 Sections on LORETTE engaged in building dug outs and emplacements	2/Lt Capt.
		6.30 pm	No 3 Section section training, and No 1 Section ANGRES Sector. No 3 Section left HERSIN to relieve No 2 Section.	
	3.7.16	3.0 a.m.	No 2 Section returned to HERSIN	2/Lt Capt.
		6.30 p.m.	Two guns placed in X.b.b.7. and X.b.b.b.5. respectively and preparations made to co-operate with raid on hostile trenches by 15th Battalion London Regt. turns registering on enemy's trenches on M.3.c and M.3.d. respectively.	Ref: Trench Map 1/10,000
		6.15 pm		
	4.7.16	1.45 am	Weather wet. Guns opened fire in conjunction with raid. Operations ceased approximately at 2.45 a.m. No. 2 Section continued section training.	2/Lt Capt.
	5.7.16		Weather wet. Dispositions unaltered	2/Lt Capt.
	6.7.16		Weather wet. -do-	2/Lt Capt.
	7.7.16	9.0 p.m.	Weather wet. No 4 Section in ANGRES Sector relieved by Section of 141st Bde. M. G. Coy.	2/Lt Capt.
LORETTE and HERSIN	8.7.16	1.45 am	No 4 Section arrived at HERSIN. Training continued	
		8.0 pm	No 2 Section left HERSIN for AIX NOULETTE and came under orders of 141st Bde. M. G. Coy.	
		11.55 pm	Three guns firing from X.b.b. joined in Artillery Barrage in conjunction with raid on M.3.b.c. carried out by 22nd Battalion London Regt.	
	9.7.16	2.45 am	Operations ceased.	2/Lt Capt.

Army Form C. 2118

WAR DIARY or INTELLIGENCE SUMMARY

(Erase heading not required.)

Instructions regarding War Diaries and Intelligence Summaries are contained in F.S. Regs., Part II. and the Staff Manual respectively. Title Pages will be prepared in manuscript.

142 M.G. Coy

Place	Date	Hour		Summary of Events and Information	Remarks and references to Appendices
LORETTE and HERSIN	9.7.16	5.0 a.m.	Weather fine	No. 2 Section returned to HERSIN	JE Capt
		10.30 pm		No. 2 Section relieved No. 1 on LORETTE	JE Capt
	10.7.16	3.45 am	Weather fine	No. 1 Section returned to HERSIN. Section training continued.	JE Capt
	11.7.16	6.30 pm	Fine, windy	No. 4 Section relieved no 3 Section on LORETTE	JE Capt
	12.7.16	3.50 am	Fine	No. 3 Section returned to HERSIN. No 1 Section carried out Range Practice at Qu...	JE Capt
	13.7.16		Dull	Section training	JE Capt
	14.7.16		Rain	Section training	JE Capt
LORETTE SOUCHEZ SECTOR and AIX NOULETTE	15.7.16	5.30 pm	Fine	Headquarters and Nos 1 & 2 Sections moved to AIX NOULETTE and took over billets of 140th Bde M.G. Coy.	
		6.30 pm		Two guns of No 1 Section took out two positions from 140th Bde. M.G. Coy at M.31 d.3.5 and M.31 d.2.1. No.1 Section at disposal of B.G.C. 141st Bde. No 2 Section in Divisional Reserve.	JE Capt
	16.7.16		Can't change to rain	Section routine.	
		11.30 pm		Co-operation with raid by 20th Battalion London Regt carried out in accordance with Appendix "A". Number of rounds fired (a) 3500 (b) 2,000	Appendix "A" JE Capt
	17.7.16		Wet	Section training carried out by Reserve Section.	
	18.7.16		Wet	" " " " "	
	19.7.16		Fine	" " " " "	
	20.7.16		Fine	10.0 pm Company came under Tactical Command of 189th Inf. Bde.	JE Capt
		9.30 pm		No 3 Section relieved No 2 Section on LORETTE	JE Capt

WAR DIARY or INTELLIGENCE SUMMARY

(Erase heading not required.)

Army Form C. 2118

142 M.G. Coy

Place	Date	Hour	Summary of Events and Information	Remarks and references to Appendices
LORETTE, SOUCHEZ SECTOR and AIX NOULETTE	21.7.16	Fine	Training carried out by Section in Reserve.	2/Lieut
	22.7.16	7.30 pm / 9.30 pm	Dull	1 Section No 2 Section relieved two guns of No 1 Section. No 1 Section relieved No 4 Section on LORETTE	2/Lieut
	23.7.16	12.30 am	Dull later fine	No 4 Section returned to AIX NOULETTE Training continued	2/Lieut
	24.7.16		Dull	"	2/Lieut
	25.7.16	11.30 am	Dull	O.C. 169th Company and O.C. No 1 Battery M.M.G. Service attended Hqs. to make arrangements for relief	2/Lieut
	26.7.16		Dull	Work continued on positions on LORETTE, and training carried out by Section in Reserve.	2/Lieut
	27.7.16		Dull	"	Appendix 'B'
				Relief carried out as per R.O. No. 1. – see Appendix 'B'.	2/Lieut
HERSIN	28.7.16	11.0 am	Fine	Company billeted in HERSIN, and under orders of 47th Division	
MONNEVILLE	29.7.16	11.0 am	Fine	Company left HERSIN and arrived at MONNEVILLE 9.0 p.m. and billeted. Came under orders of 142 Inf. Bde. Preparations made for move on 30th and foot inspection held	map Ref.
MAGNICOURT SUR CANCHE	30.7.16	8.55 am	Fine	Company left MONNEVILLE, arriving at Brigade starting point (cross Roads S. of E. in MONCHY-BRETON at 9.10 a.m. and proceeded from there in Brigade column to LENS' 11	2/Lieut
	31.7.16	10.30 am	Fine	MAGNICOURT-SUR-CANCHE Company billeted Interior Economy	2/Lieut

E.J. Barnes
CAPTAIN
142 M.G.C.

SECRET   COPY No 2

Appendix A.

142nd Bde. M.G. Coy.

Operation Order No 2

16/7/16

REFERENCE. Trench Map 1/10,000.

1. On night of 16/17 July 1916 following cooperation will be carried out by No 1. Section, in conjunction with raid on enemy's trenches at M.32.c.90.25.

2. Two guns will fire in short bursts as follows:-
   Position   TARGET
   (a) M.31.d.u.8   M.26.d (Communication trenches)
   (b) M.31.d.05.95   M.26.b (—do—   )

3. Zero will be notified later.

4. Fire will synchronise with Artillery barrage.

5. Signals. Two white rockets fired from left Bn. H.Q. will signify that Artillery and trench mortar fire is no longer required.

6. Operations will cease about Zero plus 40.

7. Guns to be in position Zero minus 60.

8. Code. Show cancelled: RAT.   Carry on: FERRET
           Barrage at once: BADGER. Stop all firing: STOAT

9. Watches will be synchronised at 8 pm.

10. Reports to Coy. H.Q.

Copy   1. File   4. No 3. Section
        2. War Diary   5. 141 Inf. Bde.
        3. No 1. Section 6. No 1. Bde. M.G.C.

                                              for O.C. 142 Coy

Appendix B.

SECRET   Copy 2

142nd Inf. Bde. M.G. Coy

Relief Order No. 1.

1. On night 27/28th. the 142. B.M.G. Coy will be relieved by 4 guns of the 189 B.M.G. Coy and 6 guns of No.1. Batt. M.M.G. Service.

2. Guides, one per gun, from positions 4, 7, 8, 5 (12) will be at SUCERIE at 10 p.m., furnished by No.1. Section.

3. O.C. No.2. Section will be at HQ Left. Bn. 7.30 p.m. to meet and conduct relieving teams to positions 13 and 12.

4. O.C. No.3. Section will be at WIRELESS Station end of COMPANY TRENCH with one guide per gun Nos 2, 3, 4, 6 at 8 p.m.

5. **ON RELIEF**
   No.1. Section will pick up its vehicles at ABLAIN CHURCH will proceed to HERSIN Q6 d.3b. and billet.

   No.2. Section (two teams) on relief will proceed to AIX NOULETTE, load their limbers and proceed with remaining two teams to HERSIN and billet. A carrying party of 12 men will report at gun positions at 8 p.m.

   No.3. Section will meet one empty limber at FRENCH DUMP at 10·30 p.m. and will proceed with it to HERSIN and billet.

6. No 4 Section will leave AIX NOULETTE at 8 pm. proceed to HERSIN and billet.

7. Headquarters closes at AIX NOULETTE at 10 pm. and reopens at HERSIN on arrival.

8. Reports to Headquarters.

9. ACKNOWLEDGE

E.C. Spencer
Captain cmdg.
142nd. Inf. Bde. M.G. Coy

Issued to signal Section 6·18 pm.   26/7/16

Copy No.	
1.	File.
2.	War Diary.
3.	No.1. Section
4.	No 2. "
5.	No 3. "
6.	No 4. "
7.	189th. Inf. Bde. (for information)
8.	142nd. " " (" ")
9.	189th. B.M.G. Coy (" ")
10.	No.1. Batt. M.M.G.S (" ")

142nd BRIGADE?
47th Division

142nd BRIGADE MACHINE GUN COMPANY

AUGUST 1 9 1 6 ::

Headquarters
142 Inf Bde.

Herewith War Diary for the month of August please.

C.E. Spencer
CAPTAIN
COMMANDING
142 M.G. COMPANY

142
MACHINE GUN Coy.
No. ✓
Date 3/9/16

WAR DIARY
or
INTELLIGENCE SUMMARY

(Erase heading not required.)

Army Form C. 2118

142. M.G.C°

Vol 7

Place	Date	Hour	Summary of Events and Information	Remarks and references to Appendices
MAGNICOURT -SUR-CANCHE	1.8.16		Company training and interior economy	
		4.0 pm	Coy left MAGNICOURT-SUR-CANCHE for MÉZEROLLES. 9 mi	
MÉZEROLLES	2.8.16	1.30 am	Arrived at MÉZEROLLES and billeted. Coy at m main road immediately S.W. of M	Map Ref. LENS 11
			MÉZEROLLES	
	3.8.16	am.	Company training	
	4.8.16	5.0 am	Company moved to MAIZICOURT	
		10.0 am	Company billeted at MAIZICOURT. Coy on main road immediately W of M on	
MAIZICOURT	5.8.16		MAIZICOURT	
		5.30 am	Company left MAIZICOURT for DRUGY	
DRUGY		10.15 am	Company billeted at Fm in DRUGY	
	6.8.16	am	Church Parade	
	7.8.16	Dull	Company training	
	8.8.16	am	— do —	
	9.8.16	am	— do —	
	10.8.16	5.0 am	Company took part in practice Advanced Guard by 21st Bde Bgp	
		late	Operations concluded	
	11.8.16	1.0 pm	Company training. Ten men lent to the Company from each Battalion in	
		am	the Brigade	
	12.8.16		Company training, at Cahedul Instruction for returned men	
		9.45 pm	Company moved to training ground ST. RIQUIER	
			ground for digging and making emplacements exercise	

28 Bonus Coll
Edge N2 M45 coy

Army Form C. 2118.

WAR DIARY
or
INTELLIGENCE SUMMARY.
(*Erase heading not required.*)

Instructions regarding War Diaries and Intelligence Summaries are contained in F.S. Regs., Part II and the Staff Manual respectively. Title pages will be prepared in manuscript.

Hour, Date, Place			Summary of Events and Information	Remarks and references to Appendices
13.6.16	DRUGY	5.30 am	Weather dull. Coy co. operated in Brigade Tactical Exercise	
		11.0 am	Interior Economy	
14.6.16		6.30 am	dull Coy moved off to training ground ST RIQUIER and took part in Brigade Tactical Exercise	
		1.15 p.m	Returned to billets. School of Instruction continued for temporarily attached men.	
15.8.16			dull. School of Instruction and Range practices carried out	
16.6.16		6.30 am	dull. Divisional Tactical Exercise	
		1.0 p.m	Interior Economy	
17.8.16			fine Company Training	
18.8.16			fine — do —	
19.8.16			dull Interior Economy	
20.8.16	BELLANCOURT	3.30 p.m	fine Coy left ST RIQUIER for BELLANCOURT	
		5.0 p.m	Company billeted	
21.6.16	BETHENCOURT	6.30 am	fine Company left BELLANCOURT for BETHENCOURT	
		1.30 p.m	Company billeted	
22.8.16	VILLERS BOCAGE	5.15 am	fine Company left BETHENCOURT for VILLERS BOCAGE	
		10.0 am	Company billeted	
23.8.16	LAHOUSSOYE	9.15 am	fine Company left VILLERS BOCAGE	
		2.0 p.m	Company billeted at LAHOUSSOYE	

Army Form C. 2118

WAR DIARY
or
INTELLIGENCE SUMMARY
(Erase heading not required.)

Instructions regarding War Diaries and Intelligence Summaries are contained in F.S. Regs., Part II. and the Staff Manual respectively. Title Pages will be prepared in manuscript.

Place	Date	Hour	Weather	Summary of Events and Information	Remarks and references to Appendices
LAHOUSSOYE	24.8.16		Fine	Company Drawing	
	25.8.16		"	- do -	
	26.8.16		Showery	- do -	
	27.8.16	5am	Wet	Reconnaissance of line by C.O. in the vicinity of FRICOURT	
		10.0 am		Church Parade	
	28.8.16		Fine	Company Drawing	
	29.8.16		"	- do -	
	30.8.16		Wet	Interior Economy and Lectures to N.C.O.'s	
	31.8.16		Fine	Company Drawing	

L.H.Spencer CAPTAIN
COMMANDING
142nd M.G. COMPANY

Army Form C. 2118.

14th M G Coy

Vol 10

WAR DIARY
or
INTELLIGENCE SUMMARY.
(Erase heading not required.)

Instructions regarding War Diaries and Intelligence Summaries are contained in F. S. Regs., Part II. and the Staff Manual respectively. Title pages will be prepared in manuscript.

Place	Date	Hour	Summary of Events and Information	Remarks and references to Appendices
LA HOUSSOYE	1.9.16	Fine	Company Training	
	2.9.16	Fine	Company took part in Brigade Tactical Exercise. Practice attack.	
	3.9.16	Dull	Church Parade and Interior Economy	
	4.9.16	Wet	School of Instruction	
	5.9.16	Dull	— do — and Field Training	
	6.9.16	Fine	To. All ranks attended Gas Test at PONT NOYELLES. Field training for the remainder of company	Ref. map. France 62 D
	7.9.16	Fine	Gun and material cleaning, and School of Instruction	
	8.9.16	Fine	Approaches to trenches in HIGH WOOD sector reconnoitred by C.O. Company carried out a route march	
	9.9.16	Fine	Small kit inspections, field training including digging	
	10.9.16	9.45 am Fine	Company left LA HOUSSOYE for MAXSES REDOUBT (E.b.a). Route AMIENS-ALBERT ROAD	Ref. map. ALBERT Combined Sheets
		2.30 pm	Company arrived and occupied MAXSES REDOUBT trenches. Transport lines established at F.1.d.	do

J. Spencer Major
Cmdg 142 M G Coy

Army Form C. 2118.

WAR DIARY
or
INTELLIGENCE SUMMARY.
(Erase heading not required.)

Instructions regarding War Diaries and Intelligence Summaries are contained in F. S. Regs., Part II. and the Staff Manual respectively. Title pages will be prepared in manuscript.

Place	Date	Hour	Summary of Events and Information	Remarks and references to Appendices
BAZENTIN LE GRAND and F.I.D.	11.9.16	2.45 am Fine turning to wet.	Coy left MAXSE'S REDOUBT for BAZENTIN LE GRAND and relieved the 1st Machine Gun Coy. Five guns in front line HIGH WOOD, remainder at BAZENTIN LE GRAND	Map Ref: ALBERT Combined Shell & Trench Map
		10.0 am	Relief completed. Artillery active on both sides. Transport lines remained at F.I.D. Dispositions 149th Inf Bde on left and New Zealand Division on right.	
	12.9.16	Fair	Heavy shelling on both sides	
	13.9.16	6.30 am Fine	No. 3 & 4 Sections relieved No. 1 & 2 Sections. Dispositions, three guns 21st Bn on left night, and three guns 24th Bn on the left in front line HIGH WOOD	
	14.9.16	7.45 am Changeable.	140 Coy. withdrew four guns in right section, and seven guns in BAZENTIN LE GRAND	
		5.0 pm	Two guns 140 section came out of the line with 24th Bn, and one gun was withdrawn from ARGYLLE TRENCH	
		6.30 pm	Last limber left BAZENTIN LE GRAND, and Coy bivouaced at FRICOURT FARM	

D.M.Baguet Major
Cmdg. 102 MG Coy

Army Form C. 2118.

WAR DIARY
or
INTELLIGENCE SUMMARY.
(Erase heading not required.)

Instructions regarding War Diaries and Intelligence Summaries are contained in F. S. Regs., Part II. and the Staff Manual respectively. Title pages will be prepared in manuscript.

Place	Date	Hour	Summary of Events and Information	Remarks and references to Appendices
FRICOURT FARM	15.9.16	5.0 am	Fine.	Ref. ALBERT. Contoured Sheet 1 Trench Map.
		6.30 am	Grenville. No 3 Section placed on immediate notice to move. 47th Div. attacked hostile trenches striking from HIGH WOOD in conjunction with 2? Div. on right, and 2nd Div. on left. Disposition of 47th Div. 140 Bde on right, 141 Bde on left, & 142 Bde in support	
		10.40 pm	Orders received to move to BAZENTIN LE GRAND	
BAZENTIN LE GRAND	16.9.16	2.0 am	Wet. Coy arrived and occupied trenches and cellars in village	
		7.15 pm	No 3 Section and one team of No 2 section retired four guns of 141 M. G. Coy occupying positions in captured German trench N. of HIGH WOOD. One team of No 2 section retired a team of 141 M. G. Coy in HIGH WOOD (S3d98)	
		9.30 pm	No 1 section took up positions in captured German trench N.E. of HIGH WOOD relieving two guns of 140 M. G. Coy. Section dug S4b S.5.	
			Usual artillery activity on both sides.	
	17.9.16	4.30 pm	Wet. Two guns of 141 M. G. Coy reported to Coy HQrs and formed Bde Reserve with ½ No 2 Section.	
		11.30 pm	O.C. No 2 Section and two guns reported to O.C. 2nd Battn. D.C. No 4 Section reported to O.C. 24th Bn. Casualties 1 O.R. Killed 1 O.R. Wounded One gun destroyed by shell fire	

WAR DIARY or INTELLIGENCE SUMMARY

Army Form C. 2118.

Place	Date	Hour	Summary of Events and Information	Remarks and references to Appendices
BAZENTIN LE GRAND	18.9.16	4.0 am (approx)	Changeable, inclined to rain.	Reference map Engins 1/40,000
		9.0 am	22nd Bn and 24th Bn carried out an attack on STARFISH trench (M34c and M35c), and the COUGHDROP (M35b)	
			O.C. No. 2 Section and two guns returned to Coy. Hqrs.	
			During the attack, No. 3 Section fired on sunken road and communication trenches left of objective	
		7.15 pm	O.C. No. 2 Section reported to O.C. 22 Bn with two guns to assist in minor attack	
		7.30 pm	No. 1 & 3 Sections relieved by 141 M. G. Coy.	
			Casualties 2 O.R. killed 1 O.R. missing 5 D.R. wounded	
	19.9.16	12.30 pm Fair	No. 1 & 3 Sections returned to Coy. Hqrs.	
		2.30 am	O.C. No. 4 Section and two guns returned to Coy Hqrs.	
		6.0 pm	Coy less O.C. No. 2 Section and one gun moved to BLACKWOOD area E.5.d.	Ref. map ALBERT Combined Sheet
	20.9.16		Slight hostile shelling of BLACKWOOD area during the morning	
		11.30 am	O.C. No 2 Section and one gun reported to Coy Hqrs having been withdrawn from the line with 22 Bn	

J.S. Spencer Major
Comdg 142 M.G. Coy

Army Form C. 2118.

WAR DIARY
or
INTELLIGENCE SUMMARY.
(Erase heading not required.)

Instructions regarding War Diaries and Intelligence Summaries are contained in F.S. Regs., Part II. and the Staff Manual respectively. Title pages will be prepared in manuscript.

Place	Date	Hour	Summary of Events and Information	Remarks and references to Appendices
BLACKWOOD	21.9.16	10 am	Coy left BLACKWOOD AREA for MILLENCOURT and billeted there. Arrived 1.0 pm	J.A.Power Major
MILLENCOURT	22.9.16	Fine	Coy dug in at D.5.a.4.5. Refitting, interior economy &c.	
	23.9.16	Fine	Interior economy.	
	24.9.16	Dull	Church Parade and Coy Training	
	25.9.16	Fine	Route March	
	26.9.16	Fine	School of Instruction	
	27.9.16	Fine to wet	Coy training and Interior Economy	
	28.9.16	12.40 pm Fine	Coy left MILLENCOURT for MAMETZ WOOD, Coy Hqrs at X.a.4.c.2.4. Brigade in support to 141 Inf. Bde in line. Coy on 2 hours notice to move. Same time at X.23.d.	Map reference ALBERT. (Corrected Sheet)
	29.9.16	Wet	Coy remained in support	
		2.30 pm	Reconnaissance of approaches to EAUCOURT L'ABBÉ carried out by C.O. Further reconnaissance carried out by Section Officers in same Area.	
	30.9.16	Fine		Map reference ALBERT
		5.0 pm	Orders received from Brigade to move to BAZENTIN LE GRAND, and to be in position there by 2.30 pm 1st prox.	

J.A.Power
Major
Cmdg 102 M.G. Coy

Army Form C. 2118.

WAR DIARY
or
INTELLIGENCE SUMMARY.
(Erase heading not required.)

142nd M.G. Coy.

Vol XI

Place	Date	Hour	Summary of Events and Information	Remarks and references to Appendices
MAMETZ WOOD	1.10.16	1.0 p.m. Fine.	Coy. left MAMETZ WOOD, arriving at BAZENTIN-LE-GRAND WOOD at 2.0 p.m. occupying trenches in vicinity Coy. HQrs S.15.a.9.12. Bde in Supports to 141 I.B.	Ref. Trench Map
		5.55 p.m.	O.C. "D" Section reported to 141 Bde in HIGH WOOD	
		11.0 p.m.	No 4 Section moved to dug-outs in BLACK WATCH trench, and formed reserve guns to 141 I. Bde	
BAZENTIN-LE-GRAND	2.10.16	1.15 am Dull	No 4 Section remained in Reserve to 141 I.B.	
	3.10.16	12.20 pm Dull	Two guns No 4 Section relieved two guns 141 Ty Coy in STARFISH LINE Remaining dispositions unchanged	
	4.10.16	4.30 p.m. Dull	No further change in dispositions. No 2 Section and one gun relieved 141 Coy at 9.30 p.m. "No 4 Section relieved by No 2 Section. Dispositions of Coy as follows:-	
			No 2 Section two guns STARFISH LINE, one gun M.29.d.1.6, one gun HIGH WOOD No 2 Section three guns O.B.1 & one gun M.29.a.1.3, Remainder of Coy BAZENTIN-LE-GRAND	
	5.10.16	Wet	Dispositions unchanged	
	6.10.16	Dull	" "	
	7.10.16	10 am Dull	141 I.B. attacked in front of EAUCOURT L'ABBE	
	8.10.16	11.40 am Wet	Lt. Negretha reported to O.C.	
		2.05 & 2.30 pm	Bns. on relieving guns at their disposal.	
		4.0 pm	Two guns under O.C. No 4 Section reported HQrs 21st Bn at STARFISH. Remaining 2 Section	

Army Form C. 2118.

WAR DIARY
or
INTELLIGENCE SUMMARY.
(Erase heading not required.)

Instructions regarding War Diaries and Intelligence Summaries are contained in F. S. Regs., Part II and the Staff Manual respectively. Title pages will be prepared in manuscript.

Place	Date	Hour	Summary of Events and Information	Remarks and references to Appendices
BRESLE-LE-GRAND	8.10.16			References French map
		9 pm	O.C. 1 reported to O.C. 2/2nd Bn M.G.C. d.S.2.	
		2.15 + 2.30 pm	Enemy attacked dropped barrage in front of EAUCOURT L'ABBÉ	
			Two guns under O.C. No 4 Section, went forward and engaged strong point unsuccessfully	
	9.10.16	10.20 am	Casualties 1 Killed, 1 Enemy, 2 Wounded O.R.	Dull
		8.30 pm	O.C. 26th S.A. M.G. Coy reported to Headquarters	
			Relief by above Company commenced	
LAVIEVILLE	10.10.16	7.10 am	Relief complete. Coy moved to MAMETZ WOOD and bivouacked	Fine
		8.0 pm	Coy left MAMETZ WOOD and arrived at LAVIEVILLE at 3.30 p.m. By	Brine. Map ref ALBERT (continued over)
	11.10.16		occupying camp	Wet
			interior economy	
	12.10.16		Inspected by Corps Commander (III Corps)	Dull
	13.10.16	1.30 pm	Transport moved off with Div Train for ST. SAVEUR by route to station	Dull
	14.10.16	12.30 pm	Coy left LAVIEVILLE for ALBERT station	Dull
		6.5 pm	entrained	
LONGPRÉ LES CORPS SAINTS	15.10.16	3.0 pm	Detrained at LONGPRÉ and marched to VAUCHELLES arriving at 7.30 p.m	Map A ALBERT/VII

Army Form C. 2118.

WAR DIARY
or
INTELLIGENCE SUMMARY.
(Erase heading not required.)

Instructions regarding War Diaries and Intelligence Summaries are contained in F. S. Regs., Part II. and the Staff Manual respectively. Title pages will be prepared in manuscript.

Place	Date	Hour	Summary of Events and Information	Remarks and references to Appendices
VAUCHELLES	16.10.16	8.0 am	Coy left VAUCHELLES for PONT REMY entraining at 1.0 pm	map Ref ABBEVILLE Bergues Sheet Ref 47
		6.30 pm	Detrained at GODWAERSVELDE and marched to camp H 4 5 (map ref 4 a 3) arriving 8.45 p.m.	
L.Z.B	17.10.16		Enterior economy & baths	
	18.10.16		Coy at Baths	Two Officers reconnoitred line at YPRES
	19.10.16	1.30 pm	Coy bombers left for LILLE GATE, YPRES	
YPRES		4.15 pm	Coy left H 4 5 for G.5.d.9.2 and entrained at 6.45 pm for YPRES	
		6.25 pm	Coy relieved 6th Aust M.G.Coy. Disposition Four guns immediate support, three guns support, four guns reserve line, four guns Ramparts reserve Coy H.Q. at I.20.d.2.1. Relief complete	
	20.10.16	11.55 pm		
	21.10.16		Dispositions unchanged. Overhead fire carried out during night by 'B' Section on roads and railways behind enemy lines.	
	22.10.16		Dispositions unchanged.	

Army Form C. 2118.

WAR DIARY
or
INTELLIGENCE SUMMARY.
(Erase heading not required.)

Instructions regarding War Diaries and Intelligence Summaries are contained in F. S. Regs., Part II. and the Staff Manual respectively. Title pages will be prepared in manuscript.

Place	Date	Hour	Summary of Events and Information	Remarks and references to Appendices
YPRES HILL 60 Sector	23.10.16	5.30 pm	"D" Section in Reserve relieved "A" Section on first defence line of defence	See Defence Scheme attached
		11.0 pm	Relief complete	
	24.10.16	Fair	Dispositions unchanged. Enemy trench mortars active during day. "D" Section on enemy roads, trenches &c.	
	25.10.16	Wet	Dispositions unchanged	
	26.10.16	2.0 am Windy burst from	Enemy unknown day and in the vicinity of Hill 60. Small bombardment ensued.	
	27.10.16	5.30pm Wet and windy	Enter section relief. "A" Section to 2nd line of defence. B Section to 1st line. "C" Section to Reserve. "D" Section to 2nd line.	
	28.10.16	Dull	Dispositions unchanged. Night firing carried out by "D" Section.	
	29.10.16	Wet	" "	
	30.10.16	Wet	Our artillery bombarded enemy lines on our RIGHT until 5.0 p.m. É enemy retaliated heavily with M. usual rifle and L.M.V. guns. D. Section fired intermittently throughout the night on bombarded area.	
	31.10.16	5.30pm Fine	"C" Section relieved "D" Section.	

B. Davies
Lt. M. G. C.
142 M. G. C.

Army Form C. 2118.

WAR DIARY
or
INTELLIGENCE SUMMARY. 142nd Machine Gun Company

(Erase heading not required.)

Vol 9/1

Place	Date	Hour	Summary of Events and Information	Remarks and references to Appendices
HILL 60 Sector	1.11.16	Fine	Dispositions three sections on the line, one section in Reserve X Trench and JACKSON STREET shelled during the afternoon	
	2.11.16	Dull	Dispositions unchanged	
	3.11.16	Snow	Dispositions unchanged	
	4.11.16 6.30am	Dull	Tornaillit shown at I.35.a.6.9 approximately	
	5.0pm		Intercom relief - Dispositions A Section Grand System, B Section Same line, C Section Same line, D Section in Reserve.	
	5.11.16	Rain	Dispositions unchanged	
	6.11.16 6.30am	Fine	Dispositions unchanged. O.C. "A" "B" "C"Coy recommitted line.	
			RAILWAY DUGOUTS slightly shelled	
	7.11.16 9.55am	Dull	RAILWAY DUGOUTS slightly shelled again with wing range.	
	6.15pm		Advanced party of 140 "C" Coy arrived with sixteen guns. Dispositions unchanged.	
	8.11.16 9.0pm	Dull	Relief by 140 "C" Coy commenced	
	11.0pm		Relief complete and Company billeted in huts at SCOTTISH LINES 62349	BELGIUM
	9.11.16	Fine	Interior Economy	Sheet 28 NW

E Davis

Army Form C. 2118.

WAR DIARY
or
INTELLIGENCE SUMMARY.
(Erase heading not required.)

Instructions regarding War Diaries and Intelligence Summaries are contained in F. S. Regs., Part II. and the Staff Manual respectively. Title pages will be prepared in manuscript.

Adams

Place	Date	Hour	Summary of Events and Information	Remarks and references to Appendices
SCOTTISH LINE	10.11.16	Fine	Section and Company Drill. Indoor cleaning &c	
G2 B. q. b.	11.11.16	Dull	Company carried out route march	
	12.11.16	Fine	Church Parade and translation of Indoor address	
	13.11.16	Fine	Indoor Recovery and route march	
	14.11.16	11.0 am Dull	Company training. Camp inspected by Divisional Commander	
	15.11.16	Fine	Company training	
	16.11.16	Dull	Coal Fatigues	
	17.11.16	8.15 pm Fine	C.O. and D.C's R.C. + D. Sections reconnoitred BLUFF Sector	
		7.0 pm	Lewis guns reduced 3 lots & 1 Group left the Camp	
	18.11.16	2.30 pm Mild	Company left SCOTTISH LINES for BLUFF Sector arriving there at 6.15 pm	
		11.0 pm	Relief complete — Dispositions — Front System — B Section RIGHT, D Section LEFT SUPPORT C Section RESERVE A Section	
BLUFF SECTOR	19.11.16	Dull	Dispositions unchanged	
	20.11.16	Fine but Windy	Dispositions unchanged. Night firing carried out on roads, tracks, and trenches behind enemy's front system.	
	21.11.16	Fine but mild	Dispositions unchanged. Night firing repeated	

Army Form C. 2118.

WAR DIARY
or
INTELLIGENCE SUMMARY.
(Erase heading not required.)

Instructions regarding War Diaries and Intelligence Summaries are contained in F. S. Regs., Part II. and the Staff Manual respectively. Title pages will be prepared in manuscript.

Place	Date	Hour	Summary of Events and Information	Remarks and references to Appendices
BLUFF SEC(OR)	22.11.16	Fine	Dispositions unchanged	
	23.11.16	Fine	Dispositions unchanged	
	24.11.16	Windy	Dispositions unchanged	
	25.11.16	Wet	Dispositions unchanged	
	26.11.16	Fine	Slight shelling of CANAL DUGOUTS	
	27.11.16	Fine	Dispositions unchanged	
	28.11.16	Foggy	Intermediate Relief - Dispositions Front System C Section, RIGHT Supports A Section, Left Supports D. Reserve B Section	
	29.11.16	Cold & misty	Dispositions unchanged	
	30.11.16	Cold	Dispositions unchanged	

E.Davis.
for Major Cmdg.
122 M.G.Cy.

Army Form C. 2118.

WAR DIARY
or
INTELLIGENCE SUMMARY.

142nd Machine Gun Co.

Vol 13

(Erase heading not required.)

Instructions regarding War Diaries and Intelligence Summaries are contained in F. S. Regs., Part II. and the Staff Manual respectively. Title pages will be prepared in manuscript.

Place	Date	Hour	Weather	Summary of Events and Information	Remarks and references to Appendices
CANAL SUBSECTOR	1.12.16		dry	Dispositions — eight guns Front System, four guns Intermediate System, four guns in Reserve.	Officers maps Cuby 1/2 10000
"	2.12.16		dry	Dispositions unchanged. One gun in Front System slightly damaged by hostile M.G. fire.	
"	3.12.16		dry	Dispositions unchanged.	
"	4.12.16		fine	"	
"	5.12.16		fine	" Band dugouts slightly shelled during the morning with L.H.V.	
"	6.12.16		fair	Dispositions unchanged.	
"	7.12.16	5.0 pm	misty	Advance party from 140 M.G.Coy arrived.	
"	8.12.16	5.30 pm		Relief of Coy by the 140 M.G.Coy commenced.	
		5.30 pm		Coy marched to Scottish Lines at 6.23 a 7.7.	
		11.30 pm		Coy billetted. One gun under a/Lt J.E. Lipper was left under the command of O.C. 140 M.G.Coy to assist in operation to be carried out by the 140 T.B.	
SCOTTISH LINES	9.12.16		wet	Internal Economy	

Army Form C. 2118.

WAR DIARY
or
INTELLIGENCE SUMMARY.
(Erase heading not required.)

Instructions regarding War Diaries and Intelligence Summaries are contained in F.S. Regs., Part II. and the Staff Manual respectively. Title pages will be prepared in manuscript.

Place	Date	Hour	Summary of Events and Information	Remarks and references to Appendices
SCOTTISH LINES	10.12.16		Weather wet. Interior Economy	G 23 a 77
	11.12.16		Elementary training & baths	
		2.30pm	all N.E. Officers returned to the day with gun team	
	12.12.16		fine & mild mist. School of Instruction	
	13.12.16		Route March & bomb throwing under B.B.O.	
	14.12.16		School of Instruction	
	15.12.16		"	
	16.12.16		fine "	
	17.12.16		"	
	18.12.16		Dull bay training	
	19.12.16		Gross Range practice carried out at DICKEBUSH Gaulle trenches	
	20.12.16	2.30pm	fine Day left SCOTTISH LINES for RAILWAY SUB SECTN	
			to 141 M Coy	
		6.00pm	Relief complete - Dispositions - Front System 5 guns, Intermediate B guns, B has 4 guns, Lynne 4 guns.	

R. B. Bruce Rogers
Cuddy 143 M.G.Cmy

Army Form C. 2118.

WAR DIARY
or
INTELLIGENCE SUMMARY.
(Erase heading not required.)

Instructions regarding War Diaries and Intelligence Summaries are contained in F.S. Regs., Part II. and the Staff Manual respectively. Title pages will be prepared in manuscript.

Place	Date	Hour	Summary of Events and Information	Remarks and references to Appendices
RAILWAY Subsector	21.12.16		Weather wet. Dispositions unchanged. Hostile artillery active in the vicinity of KNOLL FARM, METROPOLITAN LEFT and S.P.9. Work on the construction of barrage emplacements was continued at I.28.a Central.	Ref. 21.12.16 BEF (Cdg. 167 M Coy)
	22.12.16	6.0 pm	fine Raid was carried out on the CANAL Subsector front by the 140 I.B. Guns of this by did not take part in these operations, but stood to until the situation became normal (6.30pm).	Reference when
	23.12.16	6.0 am to 9.0 pm	fine, very windy Hostile artillery active generally. Construction of emplacements continued at I.28.a Central. Indirect fire was carried out by three guns firing from I.28.a 3.9, I.28.a.10.59, I.23.c.20.05 respectively on hostile trenches, dugouts and tramways. (No. of Rounds fired 2750).	
	24.12.16		fine Hostile artillery very active throughout the morning. Enemy obtained direct hit on emplacement at I.28.a 9.15. Casualties 2 O.R Killed, 1 O.R Wounded. Work continued on barrage emplacements. Night firing continued from guns at I.28.a 3.9, I.28.a 10.1, + I.23.c 20.05 on enemy roads, tramways and dugout lines. No of Rounds 3,500	Reference when Cdg in 167 MCoy
	25.12.16			

Army Form C. 2118.

WAR DIARY
or
INTELLIGENCE SUMMARY.
(Erase heading not required.)

Place	Date	Hour	Summary of Events and Information	Remarks and references to Appendices
RAILWAY DUGOUTS	25.12.16		Weather fine. Enemy unusually quiet. Dispositions unchanged. Night firing continued. No. of rounds 3000.	Reference map: Kemmel 28. N.E.S.W.
RAILWAY Sidings	26.12.16		Weather fine. Very little artillery activity. Construction of emplacements and improvement of trenches continued. Intimation of relief carried out.	
		4.30pm	Relief complete.	
		10.30pm		
	27.12.16		Hostile shelling returned throughout the sector. Construction work re carried on.	
		6.0pm	Night firing carried out from T.23.c.20.05 on hostile trench.	
		8.30am	Temporary No. of Rounds 750.	
	28.12.16	10.0pm	Shell recently of KNOLL FARM shelled. Construction of emplacements continued.	
		11.0pm		
		10.30pm	Night firing carried out from T.23.c.20.05 as above. No. of Rds 750	
		2.0 am		
	29.12.16		Weather fine. Hostile artillery has active than usual. Improvement work carried on, and the curtains fitted to dug outs.	

WAR DIARY
or
INTELLIGENCE SUMMARY.
(Erase heading not required.)

Army Form C. 2118.

Place	Date	Hour	Summary of Events and Information	Remarks and references to Appendices
RAILWAY Subsector	29.12.16 (contd)	6.0 pm 6.45 pm 6.0 pm 11.0 pm	Indirect fire carried out from I25b to 6.6.60. No of Rounds 1000 " " I25c 20.05 " " 750 " " " " " "	J.J.Spencer Major Cmdg 1/42 MGCoy
	30.12.16		Weather fine. RAILWAY Dugouts heavily shelled during the morning with L.H.V. Hostile artillery generally active in the Sector. Repair and drainage work continued.	
	31.12.16	4.30 pm 6.0 pm	Hostile artillery normally active. Construction & repair work continued. Dispositions unchanged. Intersection delay carried out & delay complete.	

J.J.Spencer
Major
Cmdg 1/42 MGCoy

WAR DIARY
or
INTELLIGENCE SUMMARY.
(Erase heading not required.)

Army Form C. 2118.

141 M.G. Coy
Vol / 4

Place	Date	Hour	Summary of Events and Information	Remarks and references to Appendices
RAILWAY SUB SECTOR	1.1.17	Weather Fine.	Hostile artillery limited to few rifle grenades and minenwerfer against the DUMP. Barrage positions in I·25·a worked on.	Expenses ends 14.1.17
	2.1.17	Fine	Enemy activity much quieter.	
	3.1.17	"	RAILWAY DUGOUTS and SHRAPNEL CORNER intermittently shelled all day with H.E. Indirect fire carried on between 6.0 p.m. and 11.30 p.m. from I·23·c·2·1. against hostile trench tramways. Number of rounds fired = 1000. Enemy artillery activity below normal.	
	4.1.17	Rain		
	5.1.17	Fine	Enemy artillery activity very much below normal. Indirect fire carried on between 9.0 p.m. and 12.0 midnight against hostile tramways. Intersection Relief carried out.	
	6.1.17	Fine to wet	Enemy artillery activity below normal. Dispositions unchanged. One gun put out of action in 3 hrs by shrapnel - casualties nil.	
	7.1.17	Fine	Enemy artillery activity and aircraft activity slightly above normal. 250 rounds fired from anti-aircraft position at RAILWAY DUGOUTS at hostile aircraft	

Army Form C. 2118.

WAR DIARY
or
INTELLIGENCE SUMMARY.
(Erase heading not required.)

Instructions regarding War Diaries and Intelligence Summaries are contained in F.S. Regs., Part II. and the Staff Manual respectively. Title pages will be prepared in manuscript.

Place	Date	Hour	Summary of Events and Information	Remarks and references to Appendices
RAILWAY SUBSECTOR	8.1.17	Weather fine.	Enemy artillery activity normal.	
	9.1.17	Rain to wet	Heavy shelling in the vicinity of METROPOLITAN LEFT and KNOLL FARM. One gun placed in Serpentine Tunnel. Dispositions now — 1 gun in Gnome system, 2 guns in Intermediate system and 3 guns in 'B' strand, and 4 guns in Reserve. Trenches and positions improved.	Reference map. Trench map 142 S.W.
	10.1.17	fine.	Hostile artillery activity below normal. Dugouts completed in METROPOLITAN LEFT.	
	11.1.17	Rain to wet	Hostile shelling and machine gunning active against the DUMP.	
	12.1.17	Rain	Enemy artillery activity below normal. Dugouts at MANOR FARM and in FOSSE WAY repaired. Intermittent L. Relief – Dispositions unchanged	
	13.1.17	mild	Enemy fairly quiet. Improvements and repairs made in S.P.10. Emplacements and	
	14.1.17	Foggy	Enemy artillery activity very much below normal.	
	15.1.17	Rain to snow	S.P.10 shelled with H.E. and L.H.V. during the afternoon dump in FOSSE WAY repaired.	
	16.1.17		Trench mortars and rifle grenades, heavy bombardment of the	

Army Form C. 2118.

WAR DIARY
or
INTELLIGENCE SUMMARY.
(Erase heading not required.)

Instructions regarding War Diaries and Intelligence Summaries are contained in F. S. Regs., Part II. and the Staff Manual respectively. Title pages will be prepared in manuscript.

Place	Date	Hour	Summary of Events and Information	Remarks and references to Appendices
RAILWAY Dugouts	18.1.17 contd		enemy front system, commencing at 7.15 am and lasting until dusk. In co-operation with the bombardment indirect fire carried on by 3 guns, one on FOSSE WAY and two in barrage positions, to flank the artillery bombardment. Rounds of ammn fired 12,250. Enemy retaliated with heavy bombardment of our front system lasting four hours	Appendices 142 –
	19.1.17		Weather Snow. Five minutes intense bombardment of enemy front line again at 1.45 a.m. – the same guns as on previous day co-operated. Number of rounds fired 3,000. No retaliation by the enemy.	
	18.1.17	"	Enemy artillery activity slightly below normal. Dispositions unchanged	
	19.1.17	"	"	
	20.1.17	"	"	
	21.1.17	"	Enemy hostile artillery quiet. Work of M.G. Tunnel emplacement in LARCH WOOD and on OBSERVATORY RIDGE continued	
	22.1.17	"	No movement hostile artillery to report. Work continued on Tunnel emplacements	

WAR DIARY
or
INTELLIGENCE SUMMARY.
(Erase heading not required.)

Army Form C. 2118.

Place	Date	Hour	Summary of Events and Information	Remarks and references to Appendices
RAILWAY Sidetrack	23.1.19	7.15 am	Weather fine. Hostile artillery and trench mortars fairly quiet. Our artillery and heavy artillery bombardment, machine gun fire as follows	Reference ZILLEBEKE Trench Map 1/10,000
			Gun Position Target No. of Rounds	
			I.28.a.56.50 I.35.a.9.9. 1500	
			I.28.a.55.49 I.35.b.4.b. 1500	
			I.23.c.15.15 I.36.d.1.5 1600	
			Work continued on Tunnel improvements	
		5.0 pm	Intersection Relief carried out	
		10.30 pm	Relief complete.	
	24.1.19		KNOLL FARM shelled slightly with 5.9 during the day. Operations unchanged.	
	25.1.19	9.0 am	DUMP bombarded with "Gun Jars". Enemy otherwise fairly quiet.	
		10.0 am	Operations unchanged.	
	26.1.19		Two guns sent to OBSERVATORY RIDGE and one gun to LARCH WOOD	
	approx	10.0 pm	to meet possible enemy operation on 27th inst.	

Army Form C. 2118.

WAR DIARY
or
INTELLIGENCE SUMMARY.
(Erase heading not required.)

Instructions regarding War Diaries and Intelligence Summaries are contained in F. S. Regs., Part II. and the Staff Manual respectively. Title pages will be prepared in manuscript.

Place	Date	Hour	Summary of Events and Information	Remarks and references to Appendices
RAILWAY Subsector	27.1.19		Weather fine.	Spencer Major Comdg 142 M.Coy
	28.1.19	12.10 pm	"	
	29.1.19	1.30 pm	Enemy not unusually active. Slight shelling experienced at the DUMP at 11.0 am. No further change in dispositions	
		6.0 pm	No unusual activity to report	
		10.45 pm	MANOR FARM slightly shelled with L.H.V. Intersection Relief carried out	
	30.1.19	10.0 am	Relief complete Short minenwerfer bombardment experienced in the vicinity of the DUMP. Work on Tunnel emplacements continued with.	
	31.1.19		Vicinity of METROPOLITAN LEFT found shelled with 5.9 during the morning. Dispositions unchanged.	Spencer Major Comdg 142 M.Coy

Army Form C. 2118.

WAR DIARY
or
INTELLIGENCE SUMMARY.

(Erase heading not required.)

142nd Mach. Gun Co.   Vol/5

Instructions regarding War Diaries and Intelligence Summaries are contained in F. S. Regs., Part II. and the Staff Manual respectively. Title pages will be prepared in manuscript.

Place	Date	Hour	Summary of Events and Information	Remarks and references to Appendices
RAILWAY Subsector	1/2/17		Weather Frosty. Dispositions – Front line system 6 guns. Intermediate System 3 guns, B line 3 guns, Rds Reports Reserve 1 gun. Divisional Reserve 6 guns (including 4th M.M.G. Battery) Enemy activity below normal.	
	2/2/17		Frosty. Enemy activity below normal	
	3/2/17		Frosty. "	
	4/2/17		" "	
	5/2/17		" " Intimidation Patrol carried out.	
	6/2/17		" KNOLL FARM shelled with 5.9 H.E. – no damage.	
	7/2/17		" Enemy very quiet	
	8/2/17		" OBSERVATORY RIDGE shelled with H.E.	
	9/2/17		" S.P. 10 shelled with L.H.V.	
	10/2/17		" KNOLL FARM and METROPOLITAN LEFT heavily shelled with H.E. – no damage. Intimidation Patrol carried out. Enemy quiet	
	11/2/17		Slight thaw in afternoon. Our artillery bombards the SNOUT, very little retaliation.	

Army Form C. 2118.

WAR DIARY
or
INTELLIGENCE SUMMARY.
(Erase heading not required.)

Instructions regarding War Diaries and Intelligence Summaries are contained in F. S. Regs., Part II and the Staff Manual respectively. Title pages will be prepared in manuscript.

Place	Date	Hour	Summary of Events and Information	Remarks and references to Appendices
RAILWAY Schreiber	13/2/17		Weather Slight thaw. Enemy very quiet — some hostile machine gun fire at night	
	14/2/17		" Enemy fairly quiet. Two hostile aeroplanes fired upon from Railway Dug outs	
	15/2/17		" Enemy quite quiet	
	16/2/17		Thaw KNOLL FARM shelled with H.E. Some hostile relief carried out.	
	17/2/17		Trench temp higher DUMP shelled and trench mortared	
	18/2/17		" MANOR FARM and S.P.10 shelled with L.H.V. in the morning	
			2000 rounds fired from S.P.10 at T.36a 15.45 (evening)	
	19/2/17		Dull no rain Enemy activity below normal. 1000 rounds fired from S.P.10 at T.36a 15.45. Section 7.0 pm and midnight.	
	20/2/17		Rain during morning Dist guns cooperated with raid by 140th Bde. Two guns firing from T.28 a 40.85 on to area T.35 d 10.70 - T.35 d 50.40 - T.35 a 20.55 - T.35 c 30.80. One gun firing from T.29 d 10.50 on O.5 d 20.98 - T.35 c 15.15 on T.36 c 10.50 (communication trench). 12.000 rounds fired in all. Enemy unjammedly retaliated on our frontage. Tripods in Infantry TUNNEL smashed. 15th M.H.4 Battery have 3 O.B. mounted.	

2353 Wt W2544/1451 700,000 5/15 D. D. & L. A.D.S.S. Forms/C. 2118.

WAR DIARY
or
INTELLIGENCE SUMMARY

Army Form C. 2118.

(Erase heading not required)

Place	Date	Hour	Summary of Events and Information	Remarks and references to Appendices
	21/2/17	Weather Misty no wind	1,500 rounds fired during day on tracked area, from FOSSE WAY and S.P.10. Enemy very quiet.	
	22/2/17	Very misty	Enemy very quiet. 6000 rounds fired on cutting and tracked area from barrage emplacement S.P.10 and FOSSE WAY. Smith Section relief. Enemy activity below normal.	
	23/2/17	Much early rain later	"	
	24/2/17	"	1000 rounds fired from S.P.10 at T36 to 15.40 between 7.0 pm and 10.0 pm.	
	25/2/17	Cloudy later	Cutting bombarded during afternoon with 4" and H.E. shrapnel. JACKSONS DUMP suddenly bombarded during the evening. 500 rounds fired from FOSSE WAY at T34 d 95.6.5 between 8.0 am and 10.0 am. 500 rounds fired from S.P.10 at T36 e 15.40 between 6.0 pm and 9.0 pm. Enemy activity normal.	
	26/2/17	Fine	"	
	27/2/17	Cloudy	"	
	28/2/17	Slight mist morning	Heavy bombardment of our front system between 10.0 pm and 11.30 pm. Smith Section relief carried out. 1 O.R. wounded.	

Army Form C. 2118.

WAR DIARY
or
INTELLIGENCE SUMMARY.

142nd Machine Gun Coy

Vol 16

(Erase heading not required.)

Place	Date	Hour	Summary of Events and Information	Remarks and references to Appendices
Railway Subsector	March 1	1917	Dispositions front System 8 guns, Intermediate 4 guns, B line 3 guns, Brigade Mobile Reserve 1 gun (12TH M.G. Battery attached) Divisional Reserve 6 guns. Mild, Bright enemy activity below normal. Intersection relief.	
	2		Dull, Mild. D SHRAPNEL CORNER and RAILWAY DUGOUTS shelled with H.E. (4.2 calibre) 1000 rounds fired from I28 b 50.60 at I35 b 30.20 during the night	
	3		Dull, showery. Enemy activity much below normal. 750 rounds fired from I28 b 50.60 at I35 b 30.20, 1000 rounds fired from I23 c 20.15 at I35 c central and 750 rounds fired from I28 b a central at I35 d 83.55 during the night	
	4		Rain during morning dull later. Wind WWSW. Enemy activity below normal. Enemy aeroplane brought down behind SP10	
	5		Wind NNE cold, some snow; very little enemy activity	
	6		Wind NNE Enemy activity much below normal. Intersection relief	
	7		Wind NE Slight frost, very quiet	
	8		Wind NE Some snow; enemy very quiet.	

Army Form C. 2118.

WAR DIARY
or
INTELLIGENCE SUMMARY.
(Erase heading not required.)

Instructions regarding War Diaries and Intelligence Summaries are contained in F. S. Regs., Part II. and the Staff Manual respectively. Title pages will be prepared in manuscript.

Place	Date	Hour	Summary of Events and Information	Remarks and references to Appendices
March	9	1917	Mild, some rain. ZILLEBEKE HALTE intermittently shelled with LHV shrapnel during day	
	10		Dull, warm. MANOR FARM shelled with HE (5·9 calibre) no damage	
	11		Dull, warm showery. MANOR FARM shelled with LHV no damage, considerable aerial activity and artillery activity above normal	
	12		Mild, showery. RAILWAY DUGOUTS shelled about mid-day with LHV.	
	13		Wind W, dull. MANOR FARM shelled with 12cm shells 3 fell, no damage, slight artillery activity	
	14		Wind W, dull. MANOR FARM shelled with 12cm shells 3 fell, no damage.	
	15		Wind N. ZILLEBEKE HALTE STATION heavily shelled between 7.30am and 1pm with shells ranging between 4·2-inch and 8-inch (delayed action) (line absolutely destroyed for a distance of 50 yards.	[signature]
	16		Wind NW, clear, enemy fairly quiet. 2000 rounds fired from I 29 c 05.73 on I 35 c central during the night	
	17		Wind west. VERBRANDENMOLEN shelled with 5·9-inch shells between noon and 5 pm. 100 rounds fired from FOSSE WAY AA portion at hostile aircraft	
	18		Wind west, dull. METRO LEFT BELLE IRVING STREET and 4711 trench shelled	

Army Form C. 2118.

WAR DIARY
or
INTELLIGENCE SUMMARY.
(Erase heading not required.)

Instructions regarding War Diaries and Intelligence Summaries are contained in F. S. Regs., Part II. and the Staff Manual respectively. Title pages will be prepared in manuscript.

Place	Date	Hour	Summary of Events and Information	Remarks and references to Appendices
March	18	1917	with #F LHV during morning. Interaction relief	
	19		Wind W, wet, dull, quiet	
	20		Wind W, dull, Back area shelled with H.E.	
	21		Wind W. METRO LEFT, X RIGHT AND ZILLEBEKE SWITCH heavily shelled between 8am and 9am with HE (4.2 and 5.9 inch calibre) B section, 141 company, relieved B section, 142 company in front system. Alteration in dispositions: A and B sections proceeded with 142 Brigade to ST. OMER. Guns in divisional reserve now 2 (MMG battery)	
	22		Wind W, dull. Artillery activity normal. 1000 rounds fired from I 25 c 20.15 at O 6 a 50	
	23		Wind W, fine. 150 rounds fired from FOSSE WAY AA position at hostile aircraft. Butting heavily bombarded between 7.30 am and 9 am with HE (4.2 and 5.9 inch calibres)	[signature]
	24		Wind W, fine. Road between LILLE GATE and SHRAPNEL CORNER heavily shelled with heavy howitzers between 5 and 6 pm	
	25		Wind NW, showery. During the night 24–25th time advanced by 1 hour to summer time. Road between LILLE GATE and SHRAPNEL CORNER shelled by heavy howitzers between 6 pm and 7 pm	

Army Form C. 2118.

WAR DIARY
or
INTELLIGENCE SUMMARY.
(Erase heading not required.)

Instructions regarding War Diaries and Intelligence Summaries are contained in F. S. Regts., Part II. and the Staff Manual respectively. Title pages will be prepared in manuscript.

Place	Date	Hour	Summary of Events and Information	Remarks and references to Appendices
March	26	1917	Wind NW, rainy. Enemy fairly quiet.	
	27		Wind W, rainy. Enemy activity normal. 1 OR wounded at OBSERVATORY RIDGE by machine gun fire. Intersector relief.	
	28		Wind W, fine, afterwards cloudy. Artillery activity normal. 1 OR wounded in STAFFORD STREET by shrapnel.	
	29		Wind W, rainy. METRO LEFT and X RIGHT shelled with HE between 5 pm and 6 pm.	
	30		Wind W, showery. Enemy activity below normal.	
	31		Wind S, showery. MANOR FARM shelled with HE (4.2 calibre) between Farm and 10 am.	

2353 Wt. W2544/1454 700,000 5/15 D. D. & L. A.D.S.S./Forms/C. 2118.

Army Form C. 2118.

WAR DIARY
or
INTELLIGENCE SUMMARY.
(Erase heading not required.)

Instructions regarding War Diaries and Intelligence Summaries are contained in F. S. Regs., Part II. and the Staff Manual respectively. Title pages will be prepared in manuscript.

Place	Date	Hour	Summary of Events and Information	Remarks and references to Appendices
Boleny	23/5		Clear day. frost. Reconnoitred Transport road with Brigdr & Steenbecque. Billetted in outskirts of town for night.	To be added to war diary from time to time. C.O.B.D.
	24		Clear day. Snowfall, wind. Sect & Coy Enclave march & Billetts at ANNEZIE, arriving 5.30pm	
	25		Clear day. Brigade raid. Centre head - army of CANZETTE 5.30	
	26		N.W.	
			Misty. Cloudy, cloudy morning. Coy Training	
	27		Snow showers - N.Wind. Coy Training	
	28		Fine day. wind [illegible]. Coy Parades.	
	29		Also dull during morning. Coy Training	
	30		dull. Some rain in N.W. Coy Parades	
	31		dull - warmer [illegible] stern - cold N.W.	

R.B. Baird

Confidential

Headquarters

142 Inf Bde

Herewith War Diary

for the month of April 1917 please

E Spencer
Major
Cmdg 142 M.G. Coy.

142
MACHINE GUN Coy.
No. ✓
Date 2/5/17

Army Form C. 2118.

WAR DIARY
or
INTELLIGENCE SUMMARY.
(Erase heading not required.)

142nd M.G. Co. 9/M/17

Remarks and references to Appendices: References notes Cuigl in. M/1/07

Place	Date	Hour	Summary of Events and Information
RAILWAY Sub Sector	1.4.17		Weather. Wind S.W. Dispositions Barrè System 9 guns, Intermediate line 3 guns, 1 B Line at HARRINGTON line 3 guns, 1 gun Brigade Mobile Reserve. (B Section 141 M.G. Coy and 4th M.M.G. Battery attached to Company). A - B Sections attached with 142 Inf. Bde in leaving at GANSPETTE. Two guns of A" M.G. Battery in Divisional Reserve. One in new dugout at OBSERVATORY RIDGE two O.R. wounded by fire.
	2.4.17		Wind W. Enemy very quiet. Intersection Relief.
	3.4.17		" S.W. Enemy activity very slight
	4.4.17		" S.W. "
	5.4.17		" W. METROPOLITAN LEFT and X Right intermittently shelled during morning.
	6.4.17		" W. MANOR FARM shelled with L.H.V. during morning. METROPOLITAN LEFT and X Right shelled with H.E. during morning. (A 19th M.G. Coy. lifted two guns on OBSERVATORY RIDGE at 11.0 p.m.
	7.4.17		" W. Enemy activity slightly above normal. Four machine guns (A/19 ZILLEBEKE) at I.28.a.5.4. and I.28.b.50.60 and one at I.23.c.2.1.) co-operated with artillery on Machine guns 18th Pn London Regt on German column at T.34.b.6.d.

Army Form C. 2118.

WAR DIARY
or
INTELLIGENCE SUMMARY.
(Erase heading not required.)

Instructions regarding War Diaries and Intelligence Summaries are contained in F. S. Regs., Part II. and the Staff Manual respectively. Title pages will be prepared in manuscript.

Place	Date	Hour	Summary of Events and Information	Remarks and references to Appendices
RAILWAY Sub Section				Ref ZILLEBEKE 1/10,000
	8.4.17		25,000 Rounds S.A.A. sent to enemy communication trenches in the vicinity of above area.	
		Weather Rainy.	Enemy activity slightly above normal.	
	9.4.17	Muddy & Snowing	The whole front System from the RAVINE to the GAP was heavily bombarded between 1.30 a.m. and 4.30 p.m., with shells of all calibres. At 6.45 p.m. enemy in greatly increased numbers was seen shelling the forward trenches with gas shells. He then made short and urgent bursts on the company frontage leading the DUMP. He demolished the dugouts and tunnels in the DUMP. Casualties 5. O.R. wounded. During bombardment all front gun positions of D Section were damaged. 23179 L/Cpl H.T. BAXTER and 44056 Pte D. FERGUSON, 9th Bn INFANTRY TUNNEL gun were called into action and they fired 300 rounds of gun was demolished, and they themselves wounded. For this action they were both awarded the Military Medal. One gun (INFANTRY TUNNEL) missing, personally exposed by the enemy. C & D Sections relieved by Sections of 10th M.G. Coy. C Section then relieved in Sections of 141 M. G. Co. in the B Line in CANAL Subsector.	I.29.C.50.35 approx

2353 Wt. W2544/1454 700,000 5/15 D. D. & L.   A.D.S.S. Forms/C. 2118.

Army Form C. 2118.

WAR DIARY
or
INTELLIGENCE SUMMARY.
(Erase heading not required.)

Instructions regarding War Diaries and Intelligence Summaries are contained in F.S. Regs., Part II. and the Staff Manual respectively. Title pages will be prepared in manuscript.

Place	Date	Hour	Summary of Events and Information	Remarks and references to Appendices
CANAL Sub Section	10.4.17	Weather	Intermittent fire and shrapnel. Dispositions – C Section (four guns) in B line, one gun in Ropple Mobile Reserve at Coy Hqts. A, B & D (minus B) Sections in Divisional Reserve. Enemy activity slight	Ref 2/4/13/RKE 1/10,000
	11.4.17	Wet.	B Section relieved Section of 141 M.G. Coy in Bank System. A Section relieved C Section in B line. One gun of C Section handed in B line. One gun of D Section moved in bank System.	Reference maps Cuff ver. hi/Coy
			Dispositions – four guns in Bank System, one gun in bankside line, four guns in B line, one gun in Ropple Mobile Reserve, one gun in Divisional Reserve.	
		Fair.	Enemy fairly quiet.	
	12.4.17	Wet.	Intermittent shelling of Bank System and back areas	
	13.4.17	"	" " " " " " " Much	
	14.4.17	"	machine gun activity by the enemy during the night.	
	15.4.17	Fair.	Enemy activity below normal.	
	16.4.17	"	Enemy comparatively quiet	
	17.4.17	"	Enemy activity slight. 500 Rounds from T.28.a.40.40 at T.38.6.60.10 T.14.6.0 RKE E.d.S.a.	

Army Form C. 2118.

WAR DIARY
or
INTELLIGENCE SUMMARY.
(Erase heading not required.)

Instructions regarding War Diaries and Intelligence Summaries are contained in F. S. Regs., Part II. and the Staff Manual respectively. Title pages will be prepared in manuscript.

Place	Date	Hour	Summary of Events and Information	Remarks and references to Appendices
CANAL Sub Sector				Ref 2/445AMC 1/10,000 22/Benses Major Cliffy 2nd M. Loy
	18.4.17	Weather	Between 8.0 p.m. and 9.0 p.m. 1000 Rounds fired from I 27 d. 40.60 on I 36 c. 10.50 to I 36 c. 30.00 between 7.30 pm and 10.0 pm Rain. Enemy activity below normal. 1000 Rounds fired from I 27 d. 34.60 at I 36 c. 10.50 between 8.0 pm and 9.30 pm	
	19.4.17	"	Wet. Enemy activity below normal. Hostile machine guns again active during the night	
	20.4.17	"	Guns S.W. corner of RAVINE WOOD intermittently shelled during the day Rain. Enemy activity above normal.	
	21.4.17	"	C Section relieved B Section in Front System. D Section relieved A Section in B line	
	22.4.17	"	Rain. Hostile artillery very quiet during the day. 1000 Rounds fired from S.P.8 at hostile aircraft	
	23.4.17	"	Rain. FRENCH FARM heavily shelled with H.E. 5.9 calibre during the morning	
	24.4.17	"	" BLAUWE POORT FARM heavily intermittently shelled with H.E. all day	
	25.4.17	"	"	

Army Form C. 2118.

WAR DIARY
or
INTELLIGENCE SUMMARY.
(Erase heading not required.)

Instructions regarding War Diaries and Intelligence Summaries are contained in F. S. Regs., Part II. and the Staff Manual respectively. Title pages will be prepared in manuscript.

Place	Date	Hour	Summary of Events and Information	Remarks and references to Appendices
CANAL Sub Section	26.4.17	Weather	Rain. Heavy shelling of BLAUWE POORT FARM and our around including the batteries and the left gun positions and our front system also received considerable attention.	[signature]
	27.4.17		Enemy activity below normal. 2nd Section of the 141 M.G. Coy relieved ten guns of this Coy in Front System and B line.	Paddy wire Sheet 28 N.W.
	28.4.17		Company in Divisional Reserve at HALIFAX CAMP (H.14 d)	
	29.4.17			
	30.4.17		Interior Economy	

E. Spencer
Major
Cmdg 141 M.G. Coy

Army Form C. 2118.

WAR DIARY
or
INTELLIGENCE SUMMARY.
(Erase heading not required.)

142nd Machine Gun Coy.

May 1918

Place	Date	Hour	Summary of Events and Information	Remarks and references to Appendices
HALIFAX CAMP	1/5/17	11.0 AM	Weather. Very fine. B.G.C. inspected Company & Transport. Enemy aircraft very active during the morning.	Map Ref. H.14 & 28.72 (Belgium - France 25) Copy of relief orders attached
CANAL Sub Sector	2/5/17		Section prepare for Relief. Coy moved into line and relieved 'A' M.G. Coy in BLUFF and SPOILBANK Subsector	I.33 & 34 Zill. 10000
		10.0 pm	Dispositions – A Section in GUN SUBWAY I.34.a 20.20 Zill. 10000 B Section in GORDON POST I.33.d 80.86 Zill. 10000 & WYTSCHAETE C Section at Coy Hqrs CANAL Dugouts I.26.a 00.30 Zill. 10000 D Section in SPOIL BANK I.33 & Zill. 10000 Relief Completed.	
	3/5/17	12.30 AM	Enemy artillery active on Back Area during the afternoon. Hostile artillery active on Front line System during the morning - machine gun emplacement in GUN SUBWAY demolished by a direct hit, dug-out has been smashed. 1 N.C.O. slightly wounded.	To Bur 105 being To Bur 105 being Report Major Elsie (being in sig)
	4/5/17		"	
	5/5/17		Enemy artillery activity quieter than usual on Front line system. CANAL Dugouts subjected to heavy hostile shelling with H.E. ammunition	
	6/5/17	6.20 am 11.50 am 2.0 am	" but windy " " A retaliatory counter battery work by both sides during the morning resuming	

2353 Wt. W2544/1454 700,000 5/15 D.D.& L. A.D.S.S.Forms/C 2118.

Army Form C. 2118.

WAR DIARY
or
INTELLIGENCE SUMMARY.
(Erase heading not required.)

Instructions regarding War Diaries and Intelligence Summaries are contained in F. S. Regs., Part II. and the Staff Manual respectively. Title pages will be prepared in manuscript.

Place	Date	Hour	Summary of Events and Information	Remarks and references to Appendices
CANAL Sub Sector	6.5.17	6.30 pm	Enemy commenced slow bombardment of SPOIL BANK Subsector for two hours.	28 Officers missing. Listed in 2 M.G. Coy.
		11.30 pm	Enemy re-opened bombardment for half an hour.	
	7.5.17	2.30 AM Weather	Bom. Hostile artillery opened up a nash bombardment lasting half an hour in the vicinity of the defence line, at the same time CANAL Dugouts was subjected to a heavy bombardment of armour piercing shells. Two guns and material were destroyed – no casualties. Enemy aircraft active soon after dawn.	
	8.5.17	Weather	Dull inclined to rain. Enemy artillery quieter than usual. SPOIL BANK shelled at 4.30 am for nine minutes. Hostile aircraft engaged by GORDON POST guns between 5.0 am and 8.30 am. 70 if rounds fired. 1500. BEDFORD HOUSE and WOODCOTE FARM shelled with shrapnel during the evening I.26.a.90.35. I.20.c.45.20 Tree. Front line system subjected to heavy bombardment also at 11.0 pm to	
	9.5.17	9.0 pm	Very fine. Back Areas + batteries shelled during the evening 11.30 pm a heavy barrage was opened on HILL 60 and the RAVINE also Enemy raided in front of Cafe Dugouts.	
	10.5.17	2.30 AM		
		4.30 AM	BLUFF shelled with H.V.H.E. Machine gun positions in G.H.Q. SUBWAY & KING STREET	

WAR DIARY
or
INTELLIGENCE SUMMARY.

(Erase heading not required.)

Army Form C. 2118.

Place	Date	Hour	Summary of Events and Information	Remarks and references to Appendices
CANAL Subsector	10.5.17	2.30 AM	S.O.S. was observed in direction of RAVINE WOOD. Machine guns from GORDON POST and GUN SUBWAY barrage enemy trenches opposite PETTICOAT LANE. No of rounds fired 11,750. Machine gun position in KING STREET destroyed. Casualties : 1 Officer wounded. 1 Sgt killed. 4 O.R. wounded. No 71574 Pte Yardley was recommended the military medal for his Gun and trajets also destroyed. positive average action during this evening.	action
	11.5.17		Weather fine. Hostile aircraft active between 5.12 AM and 8 C AM. 8000 rounds fired from GORDON POST anti-aircraft position. NORFOLK BANK and BEES STREET subjected to a bombardment of L.H.V. during the early morning. Hostile artillery quite than usual the rest of the day.	
	12.5.17		Very fine. Double artillery quieter than usual in the front line system but a certain amount of hostile shelling on Back Areas. A Sickness sent Nº 2 D. Sections relieved by 18 Sections of "B" M.G. Coy in GUN SUBWAY and SPOIL BANK	
	13.5.17	11.0 am 4.30 AM	Relief completed. Sections proceeded to new camp at OUDERDOM	

Army Form C. 2118.

WAR DIARY
or
INTELLIGENCE SUMMARY.
(Erase heading not required.)

Instructions regarding War Diaries and Intelligence Summaries are contained in F. S. Regs., Part II. and the Staff Manual respectively. Title pages will be prepared in manuscript.

Place	Date	Hour	Summary of Events and Information	Remarks and references to Appendices
CANAL Subsect	13.5.17		Remainder of D Section relieved from SPOIL BANK. Guns under control of B & C Sections.	
	14.5.17	9.0 AM to 3.30 PM	Hostile artillery fairly active. Counter battery activity during the evening by both sides. Sections in Brigade Reserve carried out School of Instruction.	
	15.5.17		Enemy activity fairly quiet. Field training carried out by Sections in Reserve.	
	16.5.17		Hostile artillery quieter than usual during the day. 6 minute battery were very active during the evening. LANKHOF FARM 1260 0510 Zuid 11550. Sections in Reserve carried out Company training.	
	17.5.17		Enemy activity shelves normal (?).	
	18.5.17	10.30 pm	C & B Sections relieved by A & D Sections on SPOIL BANK and GORDON POST respectively. Enemy activity during the evening fairly quiet, but slightly above normal during the evening on front lines.	relief orders attached

Army Form C. 2118.

WAR DIARY
or
INTELLIGENCE SUMMARY.

(Erase heading not required.)

Instructions regarding War Diaries and Intelligence Summaries are contained in F. S. Regs., Part II. and the Staff Manual respectively. Title pages will be prepared in manuscript.

Place	Date	Hour	Summary of Events and Information	Remarks and references to Appendices
CANAL Embankment	19.5.17	1.30 a.m	Wind. Rind. Relief completed. Sections proceeded to Camp 17 DUDERDOM.	
		5.0 p.m to 5.30 p.m	LANKHOF FARM subjected to heavy bombardment. Considerable enemy battery activity on both sides. Sections in Reserve carried out Routine Inspections.	
	20.5.17		Bombarde shelling on the SPOIL BANK and BLUFF. Extensive shelling during the afternoon. Hostile machine gun action ????? upon midnight to dawn. GORDON POST anti-aircraft gun fired at hostile aircraft. Aerial activity considerable on British side. Enemy machine swept down on its own lines. Two of our machines collided and came down in the vicinity of BEDFORD HOUSE. Sections in Reserve unaffected by the D.O. at 9.30 a.m.	
	21.5.17	4.30 p.m 10.30 p.m	Rain. Front line system subjected to rapid bombardment. 2 f Battn bombs. Regt carried out small raid on enemy sap in front of BLUFF craters. Sap found unoccupied. Sections in Reserve - field training.	
	22.5.17	3.0 a.m to 2.30 a.m	Wet. PALMI and SPOIL BANK Subactions very heavily shelled. Machine gun position in KING STREET and SUNSET SUBWAY destroyed - two guns damaged.	

Army Form C. 2118.

WAR DIARY
or
INTELLIGENCE SUMMARY.
(Erase heading not required.)

Place	Date	Hour	Summary of Events and Information	Remarks and references to Appendices
Canal Subsector	22.5.17		Night firing carried out by GORDON POST guns on hostile communication trenches from dusk to early dawn.	
	23.5.17	5.0 am to 11.30 pm	Company Sgt. Major moved from CANAL dugouts to the BLUFF (UNION SUBWAY). Section in Reserve = route march. Bns. Hostile artillery again very active N and S of the CANAL. Enemy bombardment was very intense, lasting from fifteen to twenty minutes, considerable counter battery work in the evening. Sections in Reserve = Field Training	
	24.5.17	1 pm to 6 am	Bns. Considerable counter battery activity on both sides. SPOIL BANK and BLUFF Subsectors subjected to heavy bombardment from 6.0 pm to 6.0 pm at fifteen to twenty minute intervals. Sections in Reserve = Company Training	
	25.5.17		Bns. Trench battery activity by both sides during the morning. Right CANAL Subsector shelled from 4.0 pm to 4.30 pm. Left CANAL Subsector shelled from 7.0 pm to 7.30 pm. Sections in Reserve = Company Training	
	26.5.17		Bns. Hostile artillery quieter than usual during the 24 hours. Shrapnel bombardment on Right Subsector at 6.0 pm. Deliberate bombardment carried out by our Trench = Field guns lasting all day. Minot operation carried out in craters in front of ST ELOI.	

Army Form C. 2118.

WAR DIARY
or
INTELLIGENCE SUMMARY.
(Erase heading not required.)

Instructions regarding War Diaries and Intelligence Summaries are contained in F. S. Regs., Part II. and the Staff Manual respectively. Title pages will be prepared in manuscript.

Place	Date	Hour	Summary of Events and Information	Remarks and references to Appendices
CANAL Bidewater	27.5.17	Various	Quiet. Hostile artillery very active during the afternoon from 3.30 pm to 5.30 pm. Both on the Front and Back Areas. Enemy appeared to be using very high velocity shells fired from guns close up to his Front line system. All roads used by transport were subjected to gun & shell shelling from 11.0 pm onwards. Night firing carried out by GORDON POST and SPOIL BANK on hostile dumps and communications.	copy of orders issued per hand Batl officer at 1.15 pm [signature] 27/4/17
	28.5.17	11.0 AM 11.0 AM	Guns. There was a considerable restlessness throughout the whole Salient. S.O.S. signals back hostile & friendly were seen to go up in several places. Our batteries in the vicinity of SWAN CHATEAU were bombarded with gas shells during the night. Night firing carried out by GORDON POST and SPOIL BANK guns on hostile trenches behind HILL 60. All harassment work were again shelled from 11.0 pm and onwards.	
	29.5.17		One gun from GORDON POST and one gun from the 13 lime SPOIL BANK were withdrawn and placed in Brigade Reserve, making eight guns in the line and eight guns in Reserve. Guns. Considerable shelling in the vicinity of the RAVINE at intervals	

Army Form C. 2118.

WAR DIARY
or
INTELLIGENCE SUMMARY.
(Erase heading not required.)

Instructions regarding War Diaries and Intelligence Summaries are contained in F. S. Regs., Part II. and the Staff Manual respectively. Title pages will be prepared in manuscript.

Place	Date	Hour	Summary of Events and Information	Remarks and references to Appendices
CANAL Salient	29.5.17		During the morning our bombardment being very intense and lasting ten minutes. This was repeated at 9.0 p.m.	Relief orders attached
		11.30 pm	C & B Sections relieved A & D Sections at SPOIL BANK and GORDON POST respectively. All roads used by transport were subjected to very severe shelling from 11.0 pm onwards.	
	30.5.17	2.0 AM	Relief completed. 5 Sections proceeded to Camp in OUDERDOM. Routine Inspections and School of Instruction carried out by Sections in reserve. During the night WOODCOTE FARM was subjected to a severe shelling resulting in the loss of two limbers, two guns and materials.	
	31.5.17		Sections C and D at Salient. Routine Inspection and School of Instruction carried out by Sections in reserve.	

M. Powers
Major
OC 89 102 M.G.Coy

No 3.

"C" Machine Gun Company, Relief Orders No I.   SECRET
by Major E. E. Spencer, Cmdg.

(1) On night 2nd/3rd May, 1917, the "C" Machine Gun Company will relieve "A" Machine Gun Company in BLUFF and SPOIL BANK subsection.

(2)   A Section will relieve GUN SUBWAY section.
      B Section will relieve GORDON POST section.
      D Section will relieve SPOIL BANK section.
      C Section will relieve section in reserve at COY. HQS.

(3) GUIDES. 1 Guide per section will meet A B and D sections at LANKHOF at 10 pm. Trucks will be waiting there to convey guns, material etc., to certain arranged places, decided by the "A" Machine Gun Company, where one guide per gun team will be waiting to take teams to their positions.

One guide will meet C section at COY HQ at 10 pm.

(4) Only trench stores, S.A.A., very lights, bombs, range charts, and orders for teams will be taken over.

(5) Sections will take up 10 belt boxes per gun, a very pistol for each gun, and all gun material and accessories, including condenser tubes and buckets.

(6) Section officers must satisfy themselves that sufficient water and ammunition is in each emplacement.

(7) The No 1 of each gun is responsible for the receipt of all fire orders including orders for barrage fire. He must not take over until these have been explained to him and he thoroughly understands them. Section officers are responsible that this is complied with.

(8) 4 additional belt boxes per gun will be brought up under section arrangements on the night of the 3rd/4th.

(9) The company will move from DEPOT at 8-30 p.m., in the following order:- A, B, D, C, HQS. An interval of 200 yds will be kept between sections. Limbers will accompany their respective sections. The C.S.M. will be in charge of HQS and its limber.

(10) The route to be taken will be via CAFE BELGE — SHRAPNEL CORNER, past BEDFORD HOUSE to LANKHOF for A, B, and D Sections. C Section and COY HQS. will leave the column at WITHUIS CAB.T and proceed independently to COY HQS.

(11) All limbers will wait to bring back material of "A" Machine Gun Company, and will convey the same to DOMINION CAMP.

(12) The signallers of this company will relieve the signallers of A Company. Your instruments will be taken up on H.Q. Limber.

(13) <u>WATER</u> Instructions will be issued later concerning this item.

(14) Code word for relief complete. SPEAKME

Copies to
1. War Diary
2. File
3. A Section Officer
4. B " "
5. C " "
6. D " "
7. Transport Officer
8. CMGO, 10TH Corps.
9. "A" M.G. Coy (for information)
10. 142 Inf. Bde.

R.J. Davies
Major
Cmdg. ℅ Machine Gun Coy

Copy No. 1 File   SECRET

"C" Machine Gun Company. Relief Orders No. 2.
by Major E. E. Spencer, Cmdg.

1. On night 18th/19th the following intersection reliefs will take place.

2. A Section will relieve C Section in SPOIL BANK
   D Section will relieve B Section in GORDON POST

3. Guides, one per gun, will meet incoming Sections at LANKHOF FARM at 10.30 pm (for D Section) and 10.45 pm (for A Section.)

4. O.C. Adv. HQ. will arrange that all guns and spare parts belonging to D Section are placed in B Section's positions so that D Section will be in possession of its own guns on relief.

5. B Section will leave one gun, spare parts etc., to be manned by D Section. C Section will leave one gun, spare parts etc., to be manned by A Section.

6. All orders, barrage particulars and range charts will be handed over.

7. Limbers will be at LANKHOF FARM at 12.30 am. 19th inst. to bring B and C Sections out.

8. Capt. C.G. Davies M.C. will be relieved by 2/Lt Lawson. All papers to be thoroughly explained before being handed over.

9. Code word for relief complete HARWICH.

17/5/17

D. Ralph Allard 2nd Lt.
for Major. Cmdg
"C" M.G. COY.

Copy No.			
1	File ✓	6	C Section ✓
2	War Diary ✓	7	D Section ✓
3	Adv. Hqrs. ✓	8	Transport Officer ✓
4	A Section ✓	9	Coy. Sgt-Major ✓
5	B Section ✓	10	Adv. Hqrs "B" M.G. Coy ✓ (for information)

SECRET   Copy No. 2

"C" Machine Gun Company, Relief Orders No 3
by Major C S Spencer, O.M.G.

1. On night 28th/29th May the following guns will be withdrawn and return with their teams to Depot, in accordance with 47th Div SCH 21 dated 27/5/17:-

    R 8a   GORDON POST   D section.
    R 13   SPOIL BANK   A section.

2. All ammunition and material belonging to these guns will be brought back. The men proceeding to LANKHOF FARM for rations will be available for assisting the teams in carrying this material to the limbers.

3. Limbers will be at LANKHOF FARM at 11.30 pm.

4. On night 29th/30th the following inter-section reliefs will take place :-

5. C section will relieve A section in SPOIL BANK
    B section will relieve D section in GORDON POST.

6. Guides, one per gun, will meet incoming sections at LANKHOF FARM at 11.30 pm (for C section) and 11.45 pm (for B section)

7. All orders, barrage particulars and range charts will be handed over.

8. Limbers will be at LANKHOF FARM at 1.30 pm (30th inst.) to bring A and D sections out.

9. Belt boxes (14 per gun) will be handed over.

10. Lt G.W. Tuten will relieve Lt Lawson. All papers to be thoroughly explained before being handed over.

11. Code word for "relief complete" PAULINE

12. Acknowledge.

                                                        B Spencer.
                                                        Major
Issued to signals 6.0 pm   O.M.G.
28/5/17   "C" M.G. Coy.

    Copy No 1 File   6 C section
         2 War Diary   7 D section
         3 Adv. H.Q.   8 Transport Officer
         4 A section   9 Adv. Hqrs. "B" M.G. Coy
         5 B section   10 St. G.O.   (for information.)

Secret.   Copy No. 1

142 M. G. Coy Instructions in accordance
with Second Army Offensive Scheme.

Ref. Map. ZILLEBEKE 1/10000   May 26 1917
           WYTSCHAET 1/10000
           Special map attached 1/5000

1. Should the Second Army Offensive Scheme be brought
into effect, the 47th Division will attack in the Centre with
the 41st Division on the Right and the 23rd Division on
the Left.

2. OBJECTIVES.
                The 47th Division will attack with the
140 Inf. Bde on the Right, and the 142 Inf Bde on
the Left.
                The attack will be carried out in two
phases. Phase 1 is shown with BLUE line and phase 2
with BLACK line.
                Frontage and objectives of the 142 Inf
Bde are shown on attached map "A".
                There will be four objectives in each phase
shown on map "A" by RED, GREEN, BROWN, and BLUE lines
in phase 1, and RED, GREEN, BROWN and BLACK lines
in phase 2.

3. Dispositions of Battalions.
    Phase 1   Frontage
    RIGHT   24th (A) Bn   YPRES - COMINES CANAL
                                        to HEDGE ROW inclusive
    LEFT   22nd (B) "   HEDGE ROW (exclusive) to
                                        point of re-entrant I.34.b.9.5.

    Phase 2
    RIGHT   23rd (C) Bn   CANAL O.4.b.9.2. - O.5.a.40.65
    LEFT   21st (D) "   O.5.a.40.65 (exclusive) to I.35.6.b.65
                                                              (VERBRANDEN
                                                                  MOLEN)

4. Attack will take place at ZERO hour on Z day – date and hour will be notified later.

5. Artillery Programme.

Attack will be preceded by a 5 days bombardment of enemy's trenches by Heavy and Field Artillery.

From "ZERO" onwards the Artillery Barrage will "creep" and "lift" to conform with advance of Infantry.

The approximate rate of lift will be 150 yards every 4 minutes during each Phase.

6. Appendices.

Appendix A. shows probable times of advance of our Infantry on the various objectives

Appendix B shows dispositions of the 142 Inf Bde for concentration and at ZERO hour. All troops to be in position by ZERO minus 60

Appendix C shows Scheme for Consolidation, Construction of Strong Points and Communication Trenches.

Appendix D Code for days and hours.

7. A Section. O.C. "A" Section will detail:-
   (a) 2 guns to be attached to 23rd Bn
   (b) 2   "   "   "   "   "   21st   "

He will control the 2 guns with the 23rd Bn and will detail a Sergeant to control the 2 guns with the 21st Bn.

8. B Section O.C. "B" Section will detail:-
   (a) 2 guns to be attached to 24th Bn
   (b) 2 guns "   "   "   " 22nd "

He will control the 2 guns with the 24th Bn and will detail a Sergeant to control the 2 guns with the 22nd Bn.

9. Reference Paras 7 and 8
   To O.C. "A" and "B" Sections

   Orders will be issued later, as to when and where their guns are to report.

   The Officers and N.C.O's in charge of these "pairs" of guns must make themselves thoroughly acquainted with the plans of the respective Battalion Commanders, under whose orders they will act.

   They must keep in the closest touch with Bn. Hqrs from ZERO minus 60 onwards.

   Arrangements must be made with Battalion Commanders for temporary accomodation for the teams as near as possible to Bn. Hqrs. so that the guns may be moved forward with the least possible delay.

   The role of these guns is to assist the Battalions in the work of defending captured positions, covering gaps in the line, or in any other way the Battalion Commander may direct.

10. D Section.   O.C. "D" Section will occupy the four converted emplacements situated in HEDGE ROW, LOVERS LANE, RAT ALLEY and PETTICOAT LANE respectively

    The role of these guns will be the defence of the Reserve Line against Counter Attack

    Section Hqrs will be in PETTICOAT LANE (present M.G. Section Hqrs).

11. C Section   O.C. "C" Section with four guns will be attached to the 101 Inf. Bde. Coy for "Barrage work.

    Orders for the Barrage work all details will be issued to O.C. "C" Section when received from O.C. 101 M.G. Coy.

    As soon as this work is completed (approximately ZERO + 30) O.C. "C" Section will move his guns into Gun SUBWAY when he will become Brigade Reserve. A guns

(O.C. 'C' Section)   He will report to Bde Hqrs on arrival.

Two guns of the Brigade Reserve will be earmarked for the occupation of Strong Points mentioned in Appendix C.

12. DRESS

   1. Officers are to be dressed and equipped exactly the same as the men. Sticks are not to be carried.
   2. Other Ranks.
      (a) Clothing, arms and equipment as issued
      (b) Haversack to be carried on the back with the waterproof sheet under flap and mess tin in cover slung outside.
      (c) Box Respirator and tube helmet
      (d) Filled water bottle
      (e) Iron ration will be carried in the haversack and unexpended portion of current days ration in mess tin

   The Pack and Greatcoat will not be carried. Instructions as to the storage of these articles will be issued later.

13. WATER.

   Stocks of water at present in line are situated as follows:-

CORD LANE	200 Gallons
HEDGE ROW	200 "
KINGSWAY BOG DUMP	200 "
RIGHT BN HQS (BLUFF)	300 "
LEFT BN HQS (PETTICOAT LANE)	300 "
NEW BN HQS (BLUFF)	400 "
NEW AID POST (SUNKEN ROAD)	400 "

   In addition to the above there will be 40 gallons in petrol tins at present M.G. Coy Hqs. UNION DUGWAY

13 Contd.

It is of the utmost importance that the necessity for returning ALL empty petrol tins to Brigade and Divisional Water Dumps is impressed on all ranks.

No man is to return from the lines without bringing at least one empty tin with him as otherwise it will be impossible to maintain the supply of water forward.

All ranks are also to be reminded that all water must be consumed SPARINGLY.

14 RATIONS

Detailed orders as regards rations will be issued later. General Instructions are as follows:—

For consumption on	Drawn from	Day
"X" day	Bn Dp. BLUFF (Iron Ration)	"W" day
"Y"	M.G. Coy Dp. UNION SUBWAY	"X"
"Z"	"	"Y"

The biscuit portion of the Iron Ration carried on the man will be issued on "Y" day for consumption on "X" day in the event of the non-delivery of rations on the evening of "Z" day.

15 Ammunition Dumps: Brigade
    (1) CORD LANE   I.34.b.0.9
    (2) HEDGE ROW   I.34.b.55.15
    (3) KINGSWAY   Bde Dump

16 Medical
    (a) Regimental Aid Posts
                        BLUFF   I.33.a.7.5
                        HEDGE ROW I.34.c.3.9
                        SUNKEN ROAD I.34.d.8.3
    (b) Advanced Dressing Station   WIPPLESS FARM

17. Evacuation of Wounded.
    (a) Stretcher Cases will be dealt with by the Batln nearest to hand.
    (b) Walking Cases will be directed to WOODCOTE FARM

It must be impressed upon all ranks that no able man is to assist the wounded back to the Aid Post or Dressing Station other than those specially detailed for the task viz. Stretcher Bearers and R.A.M.C. personnel.

18. R.E. Stores
    SUNKEN ROAD   I 34 a 9.9.
    CHESTER FARM   I 33 a 6.6.

Picks and shovels may be drawn from these Dumps

19. Prisoners of War
Should any prisoners fall into the hands of Machine Gunners they will be handed over to the nearest Infantry Officer with the least possible delay, after having had their arms taken from them.

20. Salvage
Whenever opportunity presents itself. Salvage must be collected and dumped in heaps either by the side of the main communication trenches or near trench tramway.

21. Papers Maps and Public Money
    (a) No papers dealing with the Scheme are to be kept in front of Bde Hqs when in the line and ALL RANKS are forbidden to discuss or enter into any conversation on the subject in public places, or at any time except when required by duty.
    (b) No public money may be carried by Officers into Bttn.

21. (b) Cont'd:

Any Officer in possession of public money will hand it in at the Orderly Room for disposal forthwith.

(c) The only maps carried by B Officers and N.C.O's taking part in the operations will be
1) ZILLEBEKE 1/10000 (German trenches only)
2) WYTSCHAETE 1/10000 -do-
3) Coloured Contour Map 1/10,000
4) Plan of YPRES-COMINES Canal
5) Diagram sketch of WHITE CHATEAU

(d) No copies of orders, documents or letters, official or otherwise, will be carried by any person on going into action.

(e) The B.A.B. code will not be taken into enemy trenches

22. Personnel left behind.

Instructions as regards personnel left behind will be issued later.

23. Points to be impressed on all ranks.
(a) The absolute necessity of carrying out all orders when times are laid down with strict punctuality.
(b) The word "RETIRE" does not exist and will not be understood by anyone in the Brigade. All ranks must be imbued with the spirit of going on to their objectives when once the advance has begun.
(c) No notice will be taken of the WHITE FLAG unless the enemy come out unarmed and with their hands up, when they will be passed through our lines as prisoners.
(d) "Trophy hunting" is strictly forbidden. This practice has been responsible for the loss of hard won positions in the past.

24. Traffic Circuits, Cross Country Tracks &c.

All information under these headings will be issued to the Transport Officer.

25. Transport

First line transport will remain at waggon lines.

A mounted orderly will report to B.T.O. at Bde Hy Transport lines by noon on Y day. S.A.A. will not be loaded on limbers, but will be kept in readiness for loading. Pack animals will be held in readiness to move at short notice but will not be betted or saddled.

26. Surplus Stores

All surplus stores, such as Officers' kits, men's pack greatcoats &c will be stored at Transport lines.

One man will be detailed as a guard over these stores.

27. Special Instructions.

(1)   Those Sections detailed to be attached to assaulting Battalions will start with teams of eight men per gun.

(2)   The loads will be disposed as follows:

   No. 1.   Tripod (less crosshead) and two gallons of water
   "   2.   Gun and crosshead; 1st aid wallet
   "   3.   Spare parts in extra haversack and 2 Belt Boxes
   "   4.   2 Belt Boxes and spare barrel
   "   5.   2 Belt Boxes, condenser tube & bucket
   "   6.   2   "   "   and 20 Sandbags
   "   7.   500 Rounds S.A.A. in sandbag, 2 Empty belts and a Broom
   "   8.   500   "   "   "   "   2   "   "   and a Shovel

   In addition each man will carry 2 Sandbags and 2 bandoliers of S.A.A.

(3)   On no account must men bunch together whilst on the move.

(4)   On arrival at position 2 men only will remain with the gun. The remainder having dumped their loads at the position will move to either flank to avoid casualties so far as possible.

(a) Spare men can be usefully employed in filling belts, collecting S.A.A. bringing back messages. &c.

(b) Officers must report to Battn Hqrs as soon as their guns are in position and should take up their quarters as near as possible to the Battn Commander.

28. The Section occupying the reserve line will man the four guns with teams of 5 including N.C.O's.
The remainder will be accomodated in GUN SUBWAY and will come under the orders of O.C. Local Reserve.
Should the Section be ordered forward these men will be sent back and the Section will move as laid down in para 29.
At each of these reserve positions there will be 8 belt boxes, 5000 rounds S.A.A. and two gallons of water.

29. Brigade Reserve Section
The guns of this Section will be manned by teams of six for the "barrage" work. The remaining 2 men per team will be accomodated at Gun Subway and will be available when the Section takes up its quarters there.

30. Forward Dumps
S.A.A. will be formed by Battalions in captured area.
As soon as possible Officers will ascertain their location from Bn. Hqs. so that time may be saved by drawing S.A.A. from these forward dumps.
Their approximate location will be the BLUE line.

31. Communication
    (a) Communication will be carried out by runners.
    (b) All reports, messages and demands for spare gun material belt boxes and reinforcements will be sent to Coy Hqs (HEDGE ROW T 34 a. 40. 05).
    (c) Duplicates of all such messages should be sent if possible via Battn relay posts.
    (d) It is highly important that reports of the situation, location of guns & Section Hqs be sent to Coy Hqs as frequently as possible.
    (e) As soon as the situation permits a runner should be sent from each forward Officer to act as runner and guide from outgoing messages and reinforcements from Coy Hqs.
    (f) The Officer i/c Reserve line guns will be accomodated at Coy Hqs.
    (g) The Officer i/c Local Reserve at GUN SUBWAY and Officer i/c Brigade Reserve of guns will be in communication with Coy Hqs by means of telephone and runners.
    (h) To prevent the attached men from being treated as "stragglers", each man will be provided with a card bearing the words "C" M.G. Coy and stating the mans number and name. This card will be carried in the right hand breast pocket.

32. Further details regarding the "Local Reserve" will be issued later.

33. Acknowledge.

E.J. Spencer
Major

27. 5. 17

Major
Cmdg 142. M.G. Coy

Copy No. 1.	War Diary	Copy No 8.	O.C. C. Section
2	File	9	" C Sub Section
3	142 Inf Bde (for info)	10	" D Section
4	O.C. A. Section	11	" D Sub Section
5	" A Sub Section	12	2nd in Command
6	" B Section	13	Depot Officer

Appendix A

Times of advance of Infantry

Phase 1

ZERO + 3 mins	Infantry prepare to leave our trenches, and where distance permits get out into "No Mans Land"
ZERO + 5 mins.	Assault 1st Objective
ZERO + 11 "	" 2nd "
ZERO + 22 "	Dispose along YELLOW line (see map A)
ZERO + 37 "	Assault 3rd Objective
ZERO + 47 "	" 4th "

Phase 2

ZERO + 3 hrs 40 mins.	Infantry prepare to leave BLUE LINE
" + 4 hrs 2 "	Assault 1st Objective
" + 4 hrs 37 "	" 2nd "
" + 5 hrs 20 "	" 3rd "
" + 5 hrs 28 "	" 4th "

Appendix "B"

Unit.	Disp. previous to ZERO – 12 hours	Disp. ZERO – 60
Bde Hq	BLUFF Tunnels EU 20	EU 20
21st Bn	WOODCOTE HOUSE	PETTICOAT LANE E.5.43
22nd Bn	PETTICOAT LANE. E543	" "
23rd Bn	BLUFF Tunnels	BLUFF Tunnels (Miners Dugs)
24th Bn	" "	" "
142 M.G. Coy	UNION SUBWAY	HEDGE ROW
142 T.M.B	WOODCOTE HOUSE	" "

Appendix C

(a) **Consolidation General Scheme**

    1. Front line on furthest position gained
    2. Reserve line on BLUE line generally

Appendix C contd.

b. **Strong Points**

1. I.35.c.15.05. to be manned by one platoon and one Lewis gun 24th Battn.
2. I.35.c.48.30. to be manned by one platoon and one Lewis gun 22nd Battn.

c. **Communication Trenches** will be dug across "NO MANS LAND as follows:-

1. Opposite the end of MACK CUT
2. " " " " HEDGE ROW
3. " " " " PETTICOAT LANE
4. " " " " RAT ALLEY

Appendix D

Code for Days and Hours

Days
```
Z day          Day on which operations take place
Y  "           One day before "Z"
X  "           Two days    "    "
W  "           Three  "    "    "
V  "           Four   "    "    "
U  "           Five   "    "    "
```
Days before "U" day will be referred to as -

Z-6, Z-7, Z-8 etc.

```
A day          One day after Z
B  "           Two days   "
C  "           Three days "
```

Days after "C" will be referred to as Z plus 4, Z plus 5 etc.

Hours on Z day

Zero is the exact time at which operation will commence and times will be registered in hours and minutes plus or minus from ZERO, even if they encroach on Y day.

Secret   Copy No. 1.

142 M.G. Coy Instructions in accordance
with Second Army Offensive Scheme.

Amendments No 1.

Para 7

Last paragraph in above will now read

"He will control the 2 guns with the 23rd Battn, and will detail his Sub Section officer to control the 2 guns with the 21st Battn."

Para 8

Last paragraph in above will now read

"He will control the 2 guns with the 24th Battn and will detail his Sub Section Officer to control the 2 guns with the 22nd Battn."

Para 10

Last paragraph will now read

The Officer i/c these four guns will be stationed at Coy Hqs. HEDGE ROW

Para 11 Sub para 3

The barrage work will be completed at approximately ZERO + 90

E.E. Spencer
Major
Cmdg 142 M.G. Coy

27. 5. 17

Issued to all recipients of 142 M.G. Coy Instructions in accordance with Second Army Offensive Scheme.

Army Form C. 2118.

WAR DIARY
or
INTELLIGENCE SUMMARY.   1/42nd Machine Gun C.

(Erase heading not required.)

Instructions regarding War Diaries and Intelligence Summaries are contained in F.S. Regs., Part II. and the Staff Manual respectively. Title pages will be prepared in manuscript.

Place	Date	Hour	Summary of Events and Information	Remarks and references to Appendices
CANAL L SUBSECTOR	1.6.17	11.30 AM to dawn	Weather fine. Hostile artillery active on back areas. 6000 Rounds fired from two guns at Gordon's Post and one gun at I 33 c 9.4 on road junctions trackets in conjunction with Divisional harassing scheme.	R4 Maps ZILLEBEKE and WYSCHAETE
	2.6.17		fine. Enemy artillery normal, but rather erratic. 6000 Rounds fired as on previous nights scheme. D Section relieved B Section in GORDON POST.	
	3.6.17		" Enemy artillery activity normal. 6000 Rounds fired as per Divisional harassing scheme.	
	4.6.17		" 5000 Rounds fired between 3.0 pm and 3.15 pm from four guns in position at I 33 a 9.4 in co-operation with artillery and machine gun barrage at Canal Bank between O.5 a.0.3 and O.5 a.0.35. 6000 rounds fired during the night in accordance with Divisional harassing scheme. Very feeble enemy reply to barrage.	
	5.6.17		" Enemy artillery activity normal. 5000 Rounds fired at red Ruins afternoon scheme between 3.0 pm and 2.15 pm. 6000 rounds fired during night in conjunction with Divisional harassing scheme.	

Army Form C. 2118.

WAR DIARY
or
INTELLIGENCE SUMMARY.
(Erase heading not required.)

Instructions regarding War Diaries and Intelligence Summaries are contained in F. S. Regs., Part II. and the Staff Manual respectively. Title pages will be prepared in manuscript.

Place	Date	Hour	Summary of Events and Information	Remarks and references to Appendices
CANAL Sub Sector	5.6.17		Weather fine	
	6.6.17		" "	
	7.6.17	3.10AM	Enemy artillery activity normal. Troops move to HEDGE ROW 2nd Army attack (see attached Report)	
	8.6.17			
	9.6.17			
	10.6.17		S.O.S. sent up at 10.45 pm, just as the enemy put down an extraordinarily heavy barrage on our front line trenches and support lines held by our own troops. Machine guns opened, firing a few rounds each, the ceasing when no hostile activity was apparent. The enemy heavily barraged our front system between 10.45 pm and 10 AM the following morning. 2/Lt G. Johnston slightly wounded but remained at duty.	
CANAL Subsector & OUDERDOM	11.6.17		141 M.G. By relieved A gun H.D. section and 3 guns H.C. section Front system, these section taking over 141 M G.Bn Battery positions in R. Trench. A & B sections moved to Camp 17 at OUDERDOM. Transport lines moved to HEKSKEN Camp near WEST HOUTRE. 8 guns of A & B sections maintained their barrages throughout the night on enemy Avenues running N. & S. through HOLLEBEKE.	

WAR DIARY
or
INTELLIGENCE SUMMARY.
(Erase heading not required.)

Army Form C. 2118.

Place	Date	Hour	Summary of Events and Information	Remarks and references to Appendices
CANAL Secteur a HEKSKEN	12.6.17		Weather fine. A & B Sections move to HEKSKEN Camp. C & D Sections passed an uneventful day, firing slow barrage as per previous night.	Ref maps 2. I SHEET 54 & W SHEET 54
CANAL Secteur a CASSELL	13.6.17		Enemy activity fairly quiet. A & B Sections moved to billets at CASSELL arriving at 9.0 p.m.	
	14.6.17		15000 Rounds fired between 7.30 p.m and 8.35 p.m on enemy strongpoints 200 yards E. of HOLLEBEKE, in co-operation with attack by 24th Division. Information being received that enemy intended to bear on counter attack at 11.30 p.m. Barrage fire was brought to bear on Sqs O6745.00 and O.12 to 45.60. Counter attack did not develop.	1739
CANAL SUBSEC. to RACQUINGHEM			A & B Sections moved to billets at RACQUINGHEM arriving 4.30 pm	
RACQUINGHEM to HEKSKEN	15.6.17		C & D Sections uneventful barrage positions on R. TRENCH at dawn and moved to HEKSKEN Camp. A & B Sections - Saturday Ceremony	
RACQUINGHEM to SILVESTRE ST CAPPEL	16.6.17		C & D Sections moved to SILVESTRE ST CAPPEL. A & B Sections Saturday Ceremony.	Ref maps HAZEBROUCK 5A

Army Form C. 2118.

WAR DIARY
or
INTELLIGENCE SUMMARY.
(Erase heading not required.)

Instructions regarding War Diaries and Intelligence Summaries are contained in F. S. Regs., Part II. and the Staff Manual respectively. Title pages will be prepared in manuscript.

Place	Date	Hour	Summary of Events and Information	Remarks and references to Appendices.
RACQUINGHEM	17.6.17		Weather fine. C. & D. Sections rejoin Company at RACQUINGHEM	Ref map Hazebrouck &c Belgium 5.1.
	18.6.17		" "some rain" Interior Economy, Company reorganization and Company training	
	19.6.17		" "	
	20.6.17		" "	
	21.6.17		" "rain in evening"	
	22.6.17		" "	
	23.6.17		" "	
	24.6.17		" " Church Parade. Presentation medal Ribbons by Divisional Commander	
	25.6.17		" "no wind" Interior Economy	
	26.6.17		" { During this period the Coy received reinforcements to complete Establishment	
	27.6.17	7.40 AM	" "up to time" Coy moved to METEREN, arrived 12.30 pm and billeted	2nd week
	28.6.17	6.0 AM	" " Relieved 122 M. & Coy in Divisional Reserve at RIDGE WOOD. Transport moved to CHIPPEWA CAMP	3rd week
	29.6.17		Fine. Interior economy. Transport move to ROSENHILL CAMP	
	30.6.17		Hot. Coy relieved 124 M & Coy. Dispositions – 1 Section Ravinedale supports of Front system. 1 Section in Intermediate line, 1 Section in BLUE or Reserve line, 1 Section in Reserve at the DAMMSTRASSE being employed on barrage & anti aircraft work.	

SECRET   Copy No 2

"C" Machine Gun Company, Relief Orders No 4.
By Major E. E. Spencer Cmdg.

1. On night 2nd/3rd June the following moves will take place.

2. D Section will relieve B Section in GORDON POST positions at 11.30 p.m. No team guides will be required.

3. On relief O.C. B Section will store his guns and material in GUN SUBWAY. The personnel of B section will return to Depot with the exception of one man who will be left at GUN SUBWAY to act as storeman.

4. All orders, barrage particulars and range charts to be handed over.

5. A section will take all its guns and material to GUN SUBWAY and return as per para 3, leaving one man to act as storeman.

6. Guns and material thus left will be carefully stored in the eastern end of GUN SUBWAY. The "storemen" must be issued with written instructions and made to understand their duties thoroughly.

7. All packs and greatcoats that are still in possession of men up the line will be collected and brought down under arrangements to be made by Lt. Tregurtha.

8. Limber detailed to bring these packs etc back to Depot will wait on the Southern side of the CANAL near the IRON BRIDGE.

9. Code word for relief complete YOGI

10. Acknowledge.

Issued to signals at 4.30 pm
2/6/17

E. E. Spencer
Major
Cmdg
"C" M.G. Coy.

Copy No 1 File   6 C Section
         2 War Diary   7 D Section
         3 Adv Hqs   8 Transport Officer
         4 A Section   9 Adv Hqs "B" M.G. Coy (for information)
         5 B Section   10 S.M.G.O.

Headquarters
142 Inf Bde.

Report on the part taken by the 142 M.
G. Coy in the operations in the CANAL SUB SECTOR on the
7th 8th 9th & 10th June 1917.

Para 1 A. On the 6th inst: the Company was disposed as follows:-
Two guns were attached to each Battalion taking part
in the Assault, and were accommodated with their
respective Battalions.

B. Four guns were disposed in 6hippoint positions in the
Reserve Line i.e. HEDGE ROW, RAT ALLEY, LOVERS LANE
and PETTICOAT LANE.

C. Four guns were disposed in the near vicinity of
LA CHAPELLE FARM for the purpose of barraging the
SPOIL BANK in O 5 b central.

Para 2.   Action of guns mentioned in A.
1. The two guns attached to the 24th London Battalion were
commanded by Lieut Tregurtha, and both these guns left
the Assembly Trench in close support of the Second Wave.
Within a few minutes of having reached the BLUE line
Lieut Tregurtha was struck by a bullet and sustained
a fracture of left arm, putting him out of action.
The right gun had taken up a position by this
time at O 4 b. 90. 40 (approx) and consolidated.
This team sustained one casualty whilst passing
through the 3rd line. This gun fired over the heads
of the Infantry whenever the enemy appeared to
contemplate a counter attack.
The left gun was led over by Cpl Mackintosh, and
accompanied the Second Wave. This team came across a
German machine gun in a shell hole between the 1st
and 2nd Objectives, there was one man with it who
left the gun and dived into another shell hole behind,
ignoring many shots that were fired at him, eventually
being taken prisoner.

Para 2 (cont'd)

After taking the lock out of the gun Cpl Mackintosh pushed forward without further opposition and took up a position approx O5c 45.45.

Cpl Mackintosh got in touch with the team guns of the 22nd & 21st London Battns to arrange crossfire in case of a counter attack. This team sustained no casualties.

3.
The two guns attached to the 22nd London Battn were in charge of Sgt Butler and Seaman in the absence of an Officer. The right gun of the two under Sgt Butler left the Assembly Trench with the First Wave with a view to missing the barrage. Sgt Butler was wounded by a German bomber just as he had passed the First Objective but managed to bring his assailant down with a revolver bullet.

A few seconds later Pte Thomson was fatally wounded in the chest by a bullet. The rest of the team under Pte ~~Thomson~~ carried on, which held up by machine gun fire from the German third line. Endeavouring to avoid the line of fire, the team then deviated first to the left and then to the right reaching a point approx. I34d. 45.40. where they still found themselves under machine gun fire.

Pte ~~~~ found Lieut Thomas in the Adv Bde Report Centre and enquired his way being anxious to push on as quick as possible and Lieut Thomas telephoned H.QCo. Sgt asking if the gun might remain where it was until the situation became clearer. As events turned out the gun was not sent forward, on account of the forward line being swamped with machine gun later in the day.

The left gun of this post was led over by Sgt Seaman. Unfortunately the details are not available as to the experience of this team whilst going over. Sgt Seaman was relieved by Cpl Thoms in the early hours of the 9th and an order to enable the former to proceed on leave. Very shortly after this relief the shell hole in which this gun had been placed received a direct hit by a large shell, putting the whole team out of action and killing Cpl Thoms. The position that Sgt Seaman took up was approx. I35c 45. 25. from which place he had a very commanding view of the enemy country. His team sustained no casualties whilst going over but the No.1 was hit whilst manning the gun

Para 2. (Cont'd)

3. The two guns with the 23rd London Batt. commanded by Lieut Dawson, who reports as follows. The general scheme was to follow the Fourth Wave as closely as possible until we reached the Second Objective. Position was then to be taken up on the SPOIL BANK N of the Canal, with a view to covering the Infantry as they crossed the Canal, to assault the 3rd & 4th Objectives. One team under Cpl Brunswick attached themselves to C Coy while the other gun accompanied by Lieut Dawson was attached to D Coy. The right of the two guns followed the assault on the rear of the Last Wave. The hostile shelling during the advance was very erratic and consisted chiefly of H.E. shrapnel. On leaving Ob.1 the no.1 of the gun was wounded in the arm, but as the team were moving very slowly there was no difficulty in re-distributing the loads.

This gun crossed the Canal with the Fourth Wave and managed to reach the other side with only one man temporarily out of action - this man rejoined them later.

The 4th Objective was found to be deserted by the enemy but as the left flank was at that time un-protected the gun was placed to protect this flank.

During the afternoon the position was heavily shelled by field guns - the gun was put out of action, one man was killed and two wounded. Lieut Dawson then attached himself with his four remaining men and assisted the Infantry.

The left gun under Cpl Brunswick passed through the 20th London Batt. line without casualties, and from this point the gun went forward with the third Wave. The team took up a position on the SPOIL BANK at approx O5 a 65.20, from which they obtained an excellent field of fire covering both flanks of the 23rd Batt. London Regt, and consolidated there. No any targets presented themselves and in spite of heavy shelling the team sustained no casualties.

4. Lieut Thomas who was killed on the morning of the 10th inst in HEDGE ROW commanded the guns with the 21st London Batt. The right gun was taken over by Sgt Trent who is now in hospital but from information collected both these guns got well forward of the Infantry on to the SPOIL BANK and Ob.1 entered, but retired on being shelled by our artillery.

Whilst in this forward position Sgt Mead captured two German machine gunners and the gun which was handed over for the time being to the Infantry. Sgt Mead got several good targets whilst in this position. After withdrawing from the SPOIL BANK the guns took up positions at O.5.a.20.95. (approx) and I.35.c.50.30. (approx) respectively, where they consolidated.

Both these guns opened fire whenever the S.O.S. went up.

Para B Nothing of interest to report regarding these guns during the first two days of the operations. They were sent forward on the evening of the 9th inst to relieve teams in the Bonnet Area.

Para C These guns carried out Barrage duties without difficulty and came into Brigade Reserve in GUN SUBWAY at ZERO + 90.

At 6.30 p.m. 9th inst two of these guns were sent forward to reinforce the BLACK line under Lieut Pakenham. An N.C.O. and two men were wounded on emerging from GUN SUBWAY, but fresh men were immediately obtained, and after having lost direction once or twice the teams arrived at the QUARRY at 9.25 p.m.

These guns took up positions at O.5.a.40.30. and I.35.c.15.00 (approx) where they remained until relieved.

Later 2/Lieut Chambers took another gun to the Forward Area and placed it in position at O.5.a.40.60. (approx)

This left one gun in Reserve which carried on indirect fire in the vicinity of OPTIC TRENCH.

Para D.

General Remarks

1. Teams of eight proved an adequate number to take forward, and the method laid down in Coy Order for the operations regarding disposition of loads gave satisfaction.

2. By collecting bandoliers from the killed and wounded the teams were able to keep up a supply of ammunition

Pan D contd

3. The forward teams managed to keep Coys informed of their movements by means of runners but communication between guns was difficult.

4. Every man played the game in every respect and the teams showed keenness in getting forward. The same applies to men attached from Battalions and the credit is due to the Battalion Commanders compliment[?] in ensuring that as far as possible good men with machine gun knowledge were sent to the Company.

E.Spencer
Major

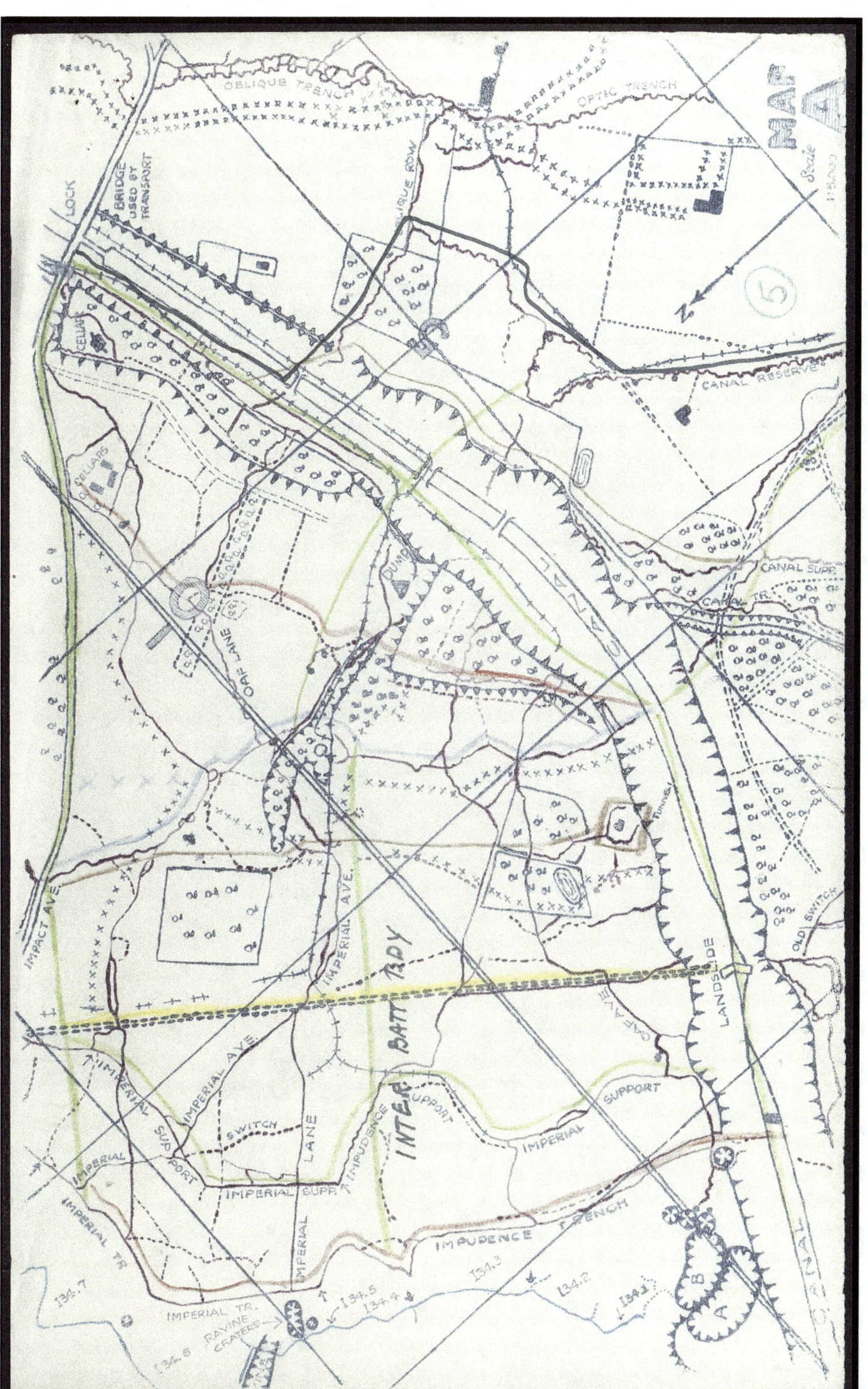

2.

C Machine Gun Company Move Orders No 5

By Major E.E. Spencer Cmdg

1. The Company will move to METEREN area on 27.6.17

2. LORRIES will be provided to take the Coy as far as SEROUS, and from thence onwards the Coy will proceed by march route.

3. RATIONS All rations with the exception of haversack rations will be carried on the lorry.

4. COOKS Ptes PIRT, OAK & NORTON, Transport Cook and Officers mess cook will proceed with stores lorry leaving at ____ and will have a meal ready for the Coy on arrival. All cookers will be taken on the lorry.

5. STORES & KIT All stores, kit and Officers valises will be dumped at Q.M. Stores by 4.15 A.M. Ptes BEAVER & ALBERT will load company lorry.

6. TRANSPORT All transport will be ready to move at 4.45 A.M.

7. BLACKSMITH Two orderlies will be detailed by Section Officers.

8. BILLETS to be swept thoroughly clean. LATRINES should be filled in over night, and are to be completed filled in & marked by 5.5 a.m. The Orderly Officer will report both billets & latrines have been inspected before moving.

9. KITS to be checked outside Coy lines by Sections. Kits which cannot go on the lorry, will be packed in the London motor Section under guards.

10. **BILLETING OFFICER.** Lt. G.W. AUTEN will report at METEREN CHURCH at 8.0 A.M. to meet the Staff Capt.

11. **GUIDE** for stores lorry. A/C.S.M. will detail one man to meet lorry at RACQUINGHEM CHURCH and guide same to Q.M. Stores at 4.30 A.M.

12. **ACKNOWLEDGE**

E. Spencer

26. 6. 17

Major
Cmdg "C" M.G. Coy

SECRET

Amendment to
"C" Machine Gun Company Move Order No. 5.
by Major S. E. Spencer, cmdg.

REF: HAZEBROUCK 5A
1:100,000

Para 1.   Add: "Leaving present billets at 5.30 am the Company will parade on Limber park at 5.20 am."

Para 6.   Add: "and will draw out of present lines in rear of 23rd Battn. transport; falling to the rear on reaching SERCUS." Order of march :— 24th Battn; 21st Battn; 23rd Battn; 142 T. M. Battery; Bde Hq.; 6th London Field Ambulance; No 4 Coy. Train; 142 M. G. Coy. The 142 Machine Gun Coy will pass the starting point (X roads 400 yards North of the "C" in SER_CUS) at 7.45 am.

Para 8.   For "6.15" read "5.15 am".

Para 7.   Add "by 4 am."

Para 13.   (Additional) "Breakfast 3.15 am; Reveille 3 am."

Para 14.   (Additional) "Acknowledge".

26-6-17

                                    N. Spencer
                                        Major
                                        cmdg.
                                    "C" M. G. Coy.

Copy No. 1 War Diary   5 C Section
       2 File   6 D Section
       3 A Section   7 Transport Officer
       4 B Section   8 4 C. of M.

Copy No 2

C. Machine Gun Coy; Move Orders
by Major E.E. Spencer Comdg

Ref: HAZEBROUCK 5A
   1:100,000

   Sheet 28 Ed. 3
   1:40,000

1. The Company with Transport will move to RIDGE WOOD area on 28.6.17, parading on Limber Park at <u>6.0 A.M.</u>

2. <u>PACKS</u> will be carried on limbers, which must be ready loaded up at <u>5.45 A.M.</u>
   <u>STORES, KITS, & OFFICERS VALISES</u> will be dumped at Q.M. Stores by <u>5.45 A.M.</u>

3. <u>LORRY</u> will move off as soon as it is packed under orders of the C.Q.M.S. The same personnel will accompany lorry as for 27th inst: and also Ptes HOWLETT, ~~ELLEY~~ HARDMAN & BEER.

4. <u>RATIONS.</u> All rations will be carried on lorry.

5. <u>TENTS</u> will be left trailed up and Camp left thoroughly clean. <u>LATRINES</u> must be filled by 5.45 A.M. <u>The Orderly Officer</u> will report these inspected before moving off.

6. <u>BILLETING OFFICER.</u> LT AUTEN will meet the Staff Captain at 8.0 A.M at Road Junction N.5.6.2.2. (Sheet 28)

7. <u>REVEILLE</u> <u>4.15 A.M</u>   <u>BREAKFAST</u> <u>4.45 A.M</u>

8. ORDER of MARCH   D. C. B. A. Sections

9. ACKNOWLEDGE

B. Davies.
Capt.
ft. Major
Comdg
C.M.G. Coy

Copy No 1 File   5 C Sect
         2 War Diary 6 D Sect
         3 A Sect   7 T.O.
         4 B Sect   8 (spare)

27.6.17

2 War Diary.

SECRET

Machine Gun Company, Relief Order N° 1
by Major E. E. Spencer, Cmdg.

Ref maps: Sheet 28 1/40,000
WYTSCHAETE 1/10,000
Secret skeleton map of
trenches 1/10,000

1. The 142 Machine Gun Company will relieve the 124 Machine Gun Company on the afternoon of June 30 and night June 30/1 July.
   1 officer, 1 sergeant, and 4 N°. 1's from A, B, and C sections will proceed up the line 29th June to reconnoitre.

2. Time-table for Section Reliefs June 30
   (a) D section will relieve reserve section in DAMMSTRASSE 2.0 pm.
   (b) C section will relieve BLUE LINE guns (Nos 9, 10, 11, and 12 guns) at 4.0 pm.
   (c) 1 subsection from A section, 1 subsection from B section will relieve front line (Nos 1 & 2 guns) and support line (Nos 5 and 6 guns) respectively. Both subsections will share one limber. time 5.30 pm
   (d) 1 subsection from A section, 1 subsection from B section will relieve front line (Nos 3 & 4 guns) and support line (Nos 6 & 7 guns) respectively, at 11 pm. This limber only will wait to carry out guns and equipment of 124 Coy.

   All above times refer to time of arrival at DAMMSTRASSE where one guide per team will be provided.

3. Guides
   Guides will be at RIDGE WOOD CEMETERY 1 hour before scheduled time to guide each section to the DAMMSTRASSE.

4. Trench Stores
   10 belt-boxes, 5,000 rounds SAA, 1 box of bombs, 2 petrol tins and orders for each position will be taken over by each team, these stores to be checked before receipt is given.

5. Concealment
   Every precaution must be taken by all ranks relieving in daylight to conceal movement and identity.

6. Information
   For purpose of relief guns of 124 Coy are commanded as follows:

7. <u>Code word</u> for relief complete "KIP" is to be sent to Coy Hqrs. as soon as sections are in position.

8. <u>Acknowledge</u>.

9. <u>Warning Order</u>
   C and D sections will relieve front system guns of 123 Coy on night 1st/2nd July. Details later.

29/6/17
          G. Eames.
          for Major. Cmdg
          "C" M.G. Coy.

Copy No 1 File
   2 War Diary
   3 A Section
   4 B Section
   5 C Section
   6 D Section
   7 Transport Officer
   8 ℅ B.S.M.
   9 142 Inf Bde
   10 124 M.G. Coy (for information).

Army Form C. 2118.

WAR DIARY
or
INTELLIGENCE SUMMARY.
(Erase heading not required.)

14 2 M.G. Coy
Vol 20

S.O. W.W.
N. Copy

Instructions regarding War Diaries and Intelligence Summaries are contained in F. S. Regs., Part II. and the Staff Manual respectively. Title pages will be prepared in manuscript.

Place	Date	Hour	Summary of Events and Information	Remarks and references to Appendices
DAMMSTRASSE	July 1		Weather, dull. Slight shrapnelling of DAMMSTRASSE during the morning. Considerable aerial activity in the evening. Hostile machines flying very low. 140th Machine Gun Company relieved the 142nd — 142nd Company relieved 128th Coy. (8 guns). Guns of 142 Company disposed as follows: 8 guns in forward system; 4 in reserve; 4 at RIDGE WOOD on anti-aircraft work. Pte Spencer slightly wounded at SHELLEY DUMP.	MAPS WYTSCHAETE 28, S.W.
	July 2		Weather; very fine. Hostile artillery active during the morning and at night in the vicinity of DAMMSTRASSE.	
	July 3		Weather; very fine. Considerable hostile artillery activity during the day. Enemy aircraft active just before dusk.	
	July 4		Weather, dull, slight rain. A & B Sections relieved 140 Company in Bonnays position at EIKHOF FARM. O.3.d.80.20. Considerable shelling in vicinity of DAMMSTRASSE at night. Sgts HERRING and SAYERS wounded.	
	July 5		Weather, bright + clear. Hostile artillery active on back areas, quiet on company sector, and SPOIL BANK O3 & 90.95.	
	July 6		Weather, bright + clear. Considerable hostile shelling at dawn and at dusk. Mostly in vicinity of OPAL RESERVE and WHITE CHATEAU grounds. Intersection relief took place after dusk.	
	July 7		Weather, fine. Our heavy artillery very active against COMINES and ZANDVOORDE. Considerable hostile aircraft activity during the evening. 3,000 rounds fired by our anti-aircraft section, no results observed.	
	July 8		Weather; dull, slight rain. Artillery on both sides very quiet until 2pm. DAMMSTRASSE shelled intermittently from dusk until dawn.	

2353 Wt. W2544/1454 700,000 5/15 D. D. & L. A.D.S.S. Forms/C. 2118.

WAR DIARY
or
INTELLIGENCE SUMMARY.
(Erase heading not required.)

Army Form C. 2118.

Instructions regarding War Diaries and Intelligence Summaries are contained in F. S. Regs., Part II. and the Staff Manual respectively. Title pages will be prepared in manuscript.

Place	Date	Hour	Summary of Events and Information	Remarks and references to Appendices
DAMMSTRASSE	July 9		Weather dull, slight rain. WHITE CHATEAU grounds heavily shelled by hostile artillery at 11 am for 15 minutes and again during afternoon. Considerable damage to trenches + ammunition buried. No casualties. Our heavy artillery bombarded enemy strong points during the afternoon. A + D sections relieved from Barrage position at EIKHOF FARM and CANAL at 5 pm by 2 section of the 140 company. At 9 pm Bosch artillery barraged enemy reserve lines. 19TH Division advanced the line on our right. 140 Bde carried out a raid on OBLIQUE TRENCH and FORET FARM, some prisoners taken. Hostile artillery retaliation severe. The company suffered no casualties. Going to shelling relief of B + C sections in forward area delayed.	Ref Maps WYTSCHAETE 28 SW FRANCE 28 SW
	July 10		Weather, very fine. B + C sections relieved by 140 Machine Gun company at 3 am and 5.30 am respectively. relief complete at 5.30 am. Sections marched back independantly to MURRUMBIDGEE CAMP, LA CYTTE.	[initials]
MURRUMBIDGEE CAMP, LA CYTTE	July 11		Weather, very fine. Company training + interior economy.	
	July 12		Weather, very fine. Company training + interior economy, squad drill + mechanism.	
	July 13		Weather, very fine. Company training; Squad drill, stoppages, PT gun drill.	
	July 14		Sultry. Company inspection by Major-General Gorringe. M.G. ribbon presented to Lt. PAKENHAM. SAA taken up to THE RAVINE, drum Stevens wounded, one mule killed.	ZILLEBEKE
	July 15		Weather, bright. Company training, elementary drill + stoppages. Lt Austen and Man 1 for A + D sections proceed to line as advance party, reference relief. "C" Machine Gun Company relieves "B" Machine Gun	

Army Form C. 2118.

WAR DIARY
or
INTELLIGENCE SUMMARY.
(Erase heading not required.)

Instructions regarding War Diaries and Intelligence Summaries are contained in F. S. Regs., Part II. and the Staff Manual respectively. Title pages will be prepared in manuscript.

Place	Date	Hour	Summary of Events and Information	Remarks and references to Appendices
	July 16 (cont)		Company north of the CANAL. Heavy hostile shelling during the night. Gas shells and H.E. shells being used. Relief considerably delayed. Pte Lancaster wounded. Guns disposed as follows: Right group, 3 guns D Section, on Triangular SPOIL BANK. Centre group B Section + 1 gun D Section in O.G. 1 opposite BATTLE WOOD and CATERPILLAR CRATER. Left group, D section on RAILWAY EMBANKMENT. C section took over Barrage positions in the RAVINE. Relief complete 11am.	ZILLEBEKE + HOLLEBEKE maps.
	July 17		Weather bright and warm. Artillery quiet during the day. Enemy opened up considerable bombardment at dusk, and carried on until dawn. Gas shells used. This company suffered no casualties.	
	July 18		Weather, dull, some rain. Enemy quiet during the day, opening up again at dusk as per previous night. Night firing carried on by guns in BATTLE WOOD, OB 1 and THE BLUFF received most attention. OB 1, on hostile strong points + tracks. 3,000 rds fires. Lt. Chanton returned from leave.	
	July 19		Weather, dull, + rain. RAILWAY EMBANKMENT at I.36.c. heavily shelled from 12 midnight to 3.30 am. Considerable hostile shelling at night. Our artillery commence intermittent bombardment of enemy positions.	S.Lt H.L of Sept 14
	July 20		Weather, bright. Considerable counter battery work in vicinity of SPOIL BANK + THE BLUFF. Have hostile bombardment from dusk until dawn. Pte Denny admitted to hospital.	

WAR DIARY
or
INTELLIGENCE SUMMARY.
(Erase heading not required.)

Army Form C. 2118.

Instructions regarding War Diaries and Intelligence Summaries are contained in F.S. Regs., Part II. and the Staff Manual respectively. Title pages will be prepared in manuscript.

Place	Date	Hour	Summary of Events and Information	Remarks and references to Appendices
	July 21		Weather dull + hazy. RAVINE shelled during the morning. 100,000 rds S.A.A. carried up for Barrage positions. D + C sections relieved by 124 M.G. Coy.	ZILLEBEKE + HOLLEBEKE MAPS
	July 22		Weather bright + clear. A + B sections relieved by 124 M.G. Coy. On being relieved sections proceeded independently to CHIPPEWA CAMP, LA CLYTTE. 2 o.r. slightly wounded during relief. Relief complete by 7am. Very heavy shelling in vicinity of THE BLUFF, RAILWAY EMBANKMENT and BATTLE WOOD, during the early morning. From 9am until mid-day neighbourhood of CHIPPEWA shelled by H.V. 6 in. gun. Company suffered no casualties.	MAP FRANCE 28 SW
CHIPPEWA CAMP	July 23		Weather hot + bright. Company training. Routine inspection + baths	
	July 24		Weather bright + fine. Company training. Barrage drill, mechanism stoppages etc	
	July 25		Wet. Company training. Routine inspection + lectures by section officers.	
	July 26		Weather fine. Company training. Barrage drill, limber packing ready for move. Fatigue party warned to proceed up the line in advance at 1am. Move postponed. Capt Davies M.C. appointed 2.O of 142 Machine Gun Company.	
	July 27		Fine; Company training. Barrage drill, squad drill, stoppages, etc. From 10 to 12 p.m. enemy aeroplane dropped bombs in neighbourhood of RENINGHELST.	
	July 28		Fine. Limber cleaning preparatory to transport inspection. Barrage drill. Enemy aircraft again	

WAR DIARY or INTELLIGENCE SUMMARY

Army Form C. 2118.

Place	Date	Hour	Summary of Events and Information	Remarks and references to Appendices
				FRANCE Sheet 28 map. HOLLEBEKE map 1:10,000
CHIPPEWA CAMP	July 29		W.K. Packing limbers preparatory to move up the line. 142 M.G. Company comes under command of 141st Division, and is detailed to occupy Barrage position near CATERPILLAR CRATER. Active at night.	
	July 30	12.45 am	Sections proceed independently to take over Barrage positions near CATERPILLAR CRATER; E Battery at I 35 a 70.55, commanded by 2nd Lt Pakenham; F Battery in lip of the crater, commanded by 2/Lt Chambers. Company in position by 4 am, 3 emplacements rebuilt + shelters made. S.A.A carried to belt-filling shelters. Some shelling during the day mainly on BATTLE WOOD and LORD LANE.	
CATERPILLAR CRATER	July 31		Weather dull, Wind NW. Zero hour 3.50 am. At 4.5 am, all objectives reported taken; 4.45 am, all objectives reported taken. Enemy Barrage mainly on front line and BATTLE WOOD. E Battery at I 35 a 80.50. (S. of CATERPILLAR CRATER had some odd shells on the trench, but no damage done. 5 am. All guns ceased fire. Slight shelling S.E. end of CATERPILLAR. Number of rounds fired, E Battery 34,000, F Battery 38,000. 5.55 pm verbal orders received from DH140 to fire on J 31 d 2 and 4; P 1 d 1, 2 and 4; and P 1 d. 5.59 pm Fire opened by all guns as directed. 6.50 pm Verbal	

Army Form C. 2118.

WAR DIARY
or
INTELLIGENCE SUMMARY.
(Erase heading not required.)

Instructions regarding War Diaries and Intelligence Summaries are contained in F. S. Regs., Part II. and the Staff Manual respectively. Title pages will be prepared in manuscript.

Place	Date	Hour	Summary of Events and Information	Remarks and references to Appendices
CATERPILLAR CRATER	July 31		message from DMGO. "Counter attack developing mainly against chinese on our left, but slightly overlapping our front." 6.55 pm Message sent to O's of G. Batteries for their information. F Battery increased fire to 1 belt per 3 minutes for 12 minutes, then resumed normal rate. 7.30 pm verbal orders from DMGO. to drop on to P1 & 2 and 3 instead of P1 & 2 and 4. 7.33 pm Verbal message sent to Lt. Pakenham to this effect. 8.30 pm Verbal message from DMGO. to slacken fire. 8.42 pm Verbal message from DMGO. to fire on P1C1, 1 Battery. 8.45 pm Guns opened fire 9. pm Slacken fire & resume normal rate of fire. 9.35 pm SOS on left. All guns opened fire on SOS lines. Rounds fired, E Battery 40,000 since 5. am. F Battery 46,000 since 5.am.	Ref. map France 28 SW

"C" Machine Gun Company Relief Orders No 8.
By Capt. C. G. Davies Cmdg.

SECRET

1. The 142 M.G. Coy will be relieved by the 140 MG Coy on the night 9/10 July 1917.

2. GUIDES Guides will be sent as follows:-

(a) A Section will send 2 guides to end of track near OLD HQ in DAMMSTRASSE at 5 pm.

(b) Section at NORFOLK ROAD will send 4 guides to SHELLEY DUMP at 5 pm.

(c) 1 guide per gun will be sent to end of track near OLD HQ and DAMMSTRASSE from each of Nos 3, 4, 7 & 8 positions at 9.15 pm.

(d) 1 guide per gun will be sent to end of track near OLD HQ and DAMMSTRASSE from each of 1, 2, 5 & 6 positions at 9.45 pm.

A guide from HQ will be sent with these guides to same place.

3. TRENCH STORES 10 belts per gun, all SAA in bulk, orders in writing for each gun, and all trench maps of this sector will be handed over. Receipts for these will be taken and sent in to Coy. Orderly Room before 12 mid-day July 10TH.

4 SANITATION. All dugouts and trenches will be left scrupulously clean and all latrines will be emptied.

5 CONCEALMENT. The danger of observation especially from high ground on north-east and from hostile aircraft will be impressed on all incoming teams.

6 DESTINATION. On relief sections will march independently to MURRUMBIDGEE CAMP at LA CLYTTE

7 TRANSPORT. 1 limber per section will be at the same rendezvous to which section guides were sent at following times:
    (a) "A" Section limber   5.15 pm
    (b) Norfolk Rd Section   5.45 pm
    (c) Limber for 3,4,7 + 8 positions
                                   10.15 pm
    (d) Limber for 1, 2, 5 + 6 positions and
           head quarters   10.45 pm

Separate orders have been issued to Transport Officer

8. RELIEF COMPLETE code word "FRAY BENTOS" will be sent by runner or by wire to COY HQ ("DMG" is position call for HQ) before each Section moves off.

9. ACKNOWLEDGE

                                                   Davies
                                                   Capt.

S.404
8-7-17.
                           Cmdg
                           142 M.G. Coy.

Copy No 1. File
        2. A sect.
        3. Norfolk Rd Sect.
        4. O.C. 1, 2, 5, + 6 guns
        5. O.C. 3, 4, 7 + 8 guns
        6. 140 Bde
        7. 140 M.G. Coy.
        8. a/CSM. + War Diary.

SECRET   War Diary   Issue No. 2

"C" Machine Gun Company, Relief Orders No. 1
by Major E.E. Spencer, Cmdg.
                                        DILLEBEKE 1/20,000
                                        HOLLEBEKE 1/10,000

1. "C" Machine Gun Company will relieve "B" Machine Gun Company north of the CANAL on the night 16/17th July 1917.

2. The relief will be carried out as follows:—

   3 guns D section   )   (F O.5.a.30.55
   forming RIGHT GROUP   ) relieve positions { G O.5.a.20.38
   under Lt. Austen.   )   (H O.5.a.50.70

   A Section, forming   )   (I I.36.c.25.30
   LEFT GROUP under   ) relieve positions { M I.36.c.15.50
   Lt. Lawson.   )   { A I.36.a.75.10
)   (K I.36.a.85.30

   B Section with 1 gun   )   (C I.35.a.70.85
   of D section under   ) relieve positions { B I.35.a.75.40
   2/Lt Hargreaves   )   { L I.35.b.50.20
)   { E I.35.a.70.80
)   (D I.35.c.20.90

   C section under   ) relieves   { Barrage section in
   Lt Pakenham.   )   (OB 1 at I.34 central.

3. GUIDES
   (a) 1 guide for D section at BRICKSTACKS at 9.30 p.m. 3 team guides will meet section at KING STREET.
   (b) 1 guide for A section at IRON BRIDGE 9 p.m. 4 team guides will meet sections at RAVINE. 1 guide for B section at IRON BRIDGE at 9.15 p.m.
   (c) C section guide 9.30 p.m. at IRON BRIDGE. 4 team guides at RAVINE.

4. BELTS
   8 belts only per gun will be taken over; 4 belts per gun will be carried up. "C" section will take up 8 belts per gun and take over 2 only.

5. WATER
   Each team should take up 1 petrol tin in addition to waterbottles.

6. LIMBERS
   1 limber per section only will be taken up. B section will take up attached gun from D section.
   Sections will be ready to move off 2½ hours before times stated for guides.

7. TRENCH STORES.

A copy of all receipts given for Trench Stores will be sent to Company Headquarters within 24 hours. Trench stores MUST be checked before being signed for.

8. PERSONNEL to be left at DEPOT

1 Lance-Corporal per section, and if possible 1 N.C.O. will be left at DEPOT with any spare men left over after completing teams of 6.

9. COY HEADQUARTERS is in KING STREET TUNNEL in the BLUFF, I.34.c.15.20.(approx)

10. CODE WORD for relief complete MIMI.

11. ACKNOWLEDGE.

C. Davies
2/Lt.
"C" M.G. Coy.

15/7/17

Copy to 1. File   6. D Section
         2. War Diary   7. 142 Inf Bde
         3. A Section   8. "B" M G Coy
         4. B Section   9. Transport Officer
         5. C Section   10. O. i/c M.

Copy No 2

SECRET

"C" Machine Gun Company, Operation Orders No 10
by Capt. C.G. Davies CMG.

I. **MOVE.** The 142 Machine Gun Company comes under orders of 41st Division from July 26th inclusive, and will move up and occupy barrage positions near the CATERPILLAR CRATER on the night 26/27th July.

II. **PARADES** "A" section will move off at 12.45 am July 27th.
"B", "C", & "D" sections will follow in order, at 10 minute intervals.

III. **ROUTE & DISPOSITION on arrival.** Sections will follow route running through DICKEBUSCH — KRUISTRAATHOEK — BEDFORD HOUSE — PETTICOAT LANE. On arrival "A" and "B" sections will form "F" Battery under command of 2/Lt. G. Chambers, and will occupy the eight positions on the lip of CATERPILLAR CRATER.
"C" and "D" sections will form "E" Battery under command of Lt. I.C. Pakenham, and occupy the eight positions 150 yards S of CRATER.

IV. **GROUP HQ** will be established in dugout at I.35.a.85.60 (in trench running down S. side of CATERPILLAR). "E" Battery Hq. in concrete dugout I.35.a.85.60. "F" Battery Hq. I.35.b.00.58. Above headquarters will be connected by telephone with D.M.G.O. at I.33.d.30.90.

V. **STRENGTH** (a) The following will be the strength of sections occupying barrage positions:—

Officers	1
Men per gun (including 2 men per gun attached from 234 Coy	6
Sergeant	1
Corporal	1
Batman	1
Total strength (all ranks)	28

(b) **Headquarters**

Signallers	6
Runners (to D.M.G.O)	2
Batman	1
Officer	1
Total Strength (all ranks)	10

EQUIPMENT

    14 belts per gun.
    4 petrol cans filled.
    Current day rations.
    2 days preserved rations.
    4 Clinometers per Battery.
    1 Belt filling machine per Battery.
    Routine gun equipment.

VII CARRYING PARTY

All available spare men will be taken up as carrying party. These men will return to DEPOT as soon as sections are in position.

VIII FIRE ORDERS

All details with reference to firing, S.A.A. supply will be issued separately to Battery Commanders.

IX ACKNOWLEDGE

25-7-17

                      A. Raines
                      Capt.
                      Cmdg
                      142 M.G. Coy.

Copy No 1 File
        2 War Diary
        3 "A" Section
        4 "B" Section
        5 "C" Section
        6 "D" Section
        7 142 Inf Bde
        8 D.M.G.O. 41st Div
        9 D.M.G.O. 47th Div
        10 Transport Officer
        11 C. et M.

WAR DIARY or INTELLIGENCE SUMMARY

Army Form C. 2118.

142nd M.G. Coy. Vol 21

Place	Date	Hour	Summary of Events and Information	Remarks and references to Appendices
BLUFF SECTOR. YPRES	Aug 1st		Wind S.W. Dispositions 8 guns at I.35.a.20.80 and 8 guns at I.35.a.82.60 in barrage positions. At 4.20am all guns fired on S.O.S. line on a barrage running north and south through HOLLEBEKE CHATEAU; fire ceased at 5.20am. 48,000 rounds fired 5.45pm All guns fired on square J.31.d. 14,000 rounds fired.	Ref map BELGIUM 28 N.W.
	2		Wind S.W. During night 10,000 rounds "harassing fire" on S.O.S. line.	
	3		Wind S.W. During night 10,000 rounds "harassing fire" on S.O.S. line.	
	4		Wind S.W. During night 10,000 rounds "harassing fire" on S.O.S. line. 1 casualty. Pte Toole slightly wounded.	
	5		Weather fine and hot. Company paraded and proceeded to ROSENHIL CAMP near RENINGHELST. In afternoon the company moved to ASCOT CAMP, WESTOUTRE, arriving at 5pm.	
	6		Fine. Interior Economy, including baths and kit inspections.	
	7		Fine. Interior Economy. Company training.	
	8		Fine. Transport moved at 8.30am to WALLON-CAPPEL area. Company training including route march.	
	9		Fine, with showers. Company entrained at 12.30pm at ABEELE; detrained at 3.30pm at ST.OMER and marched to billets at BARBINGHEM.	
	10		Fine. Interior Economy.	
	11		Fine. Interior Economy, including Company training. 3 O.R. reinforcements arrived from Base.	
	12		Fine. Church Parade at 11.10am. 1 O.R. reinforcement arrived from Base.	

Army Form C. 2118.

WAR DIARY
or
INTELLIGENCE SUMMARY.
(Erase heading not required.)

Instructions regarding War Diaries and Intelligence Summaries are contained in F. S. Regs., Part II. and the Staff Manual respectively. Title pages will be prepared in manuscript.

Place	Date	Hour	Summary of Events and Information	Remarks and references to Appendices
	Aug 13		Dull. Company training	
	" 14		Dull. Company training	
	" 15		Dull. Company training	
	" 16		Fine. Range practice from 7am to 10am. 2nd line transport proceeded with Brigade Column by road to NOORDSCHOOTE.	Ref BELGIUM HAZEBROUCK 5a
	" 17	4.15 pm	Company paraded to march to WIZERNES. 2nd line transport moved to DOMINION AREA.	
	" 18	2.55 am	Fine. Entrained 2.55 am at WIZERNES; detrained at POPERINGHE 9.40 am, and marched to SCOTTISH LINES, arriving at 12.15 pm.	
	" 19	11.50 pm	Fine. Intense enemy. Company moved to SWAN CHATEAU near YPRES arriving 11.50 pm. Company in Divisional reserve.	
	" 20		Fine. Intense enemy.	
	" 21	8 pm	Fine. Company marched into Barrage position between J7c 6.4 and J18 a 9.7. 1 OR wounded.	
	" 22	7 am	Fine. At 7am 14th Division (on our right) attacked GLENCORSE WOOD and INVERNESS COPSE. Company fired barrage on (J15 a 9.6.9.0) area round BLACK WATCH CORNER (J15 a 9.5.90) 70,000 rds fired. Enemy heavily barraged BELLEWARDE RIDGE and valley south. 2 guns knocked out. Casualties 3 OR killed 14 OR wounded.	

WAR DIARY
or
INTELLIGENCE SUMMARY.

(Erase heading not required.)

Army Form C. 2118.

Place	Date	Hour	Summary of Events and Information	Remarks and references to Appendices
	Aug 25th		Company evacuated positions at 5am and returned to SWAN CHATEAU. Guns cleaned. Kit inspection. B section proceeded; 2 guns to CHATEAU WOOD; 2 guns to front line (J8c 26.90 and J8c 30.90), to relieve 4 guns of 49th Machine Gun Company. 3 O.R. wounded.	
	25		Fine. Company relieved 12 guns of 141st Machine Gun Company in Railway Wood sector, 2 guns in CHATEAU WOOD moved up to relieve 2 guns of 42nd M.G. Coy at J8c 15.60 and J8c 26.65. Disposition 12 guns in front system; 4 guns in barrage positions at J1c.15.20.	
	26th		Fine. Intermittent shelling on front system + back area throughout the night. enemy intermittently shelled the MENIN ROAD between BIRR CROSS ROADS and HELLFIRE CORNER.	
	27th		Wet. Between 1.30 pm and 7.30 pm 4 guns at J1c 15.20 fired 24,000 rds on D.26.C. in co-operation with attack by 16th Division on our left. 1 O.R. wounded.	
	28th		Wet. Enemy intermittently shelled front system and BELLEWARDE RIDGE, occasionally with intensity; after 6pm and throughout the night, enemy shelled tracks in back area and the MENIN ROAD intermittently. 1 O.R. wounded.	
	29		Wet. Hostile shelling of WESTHOEK grew intense at 5.10am and 7.30 pm lasting for 15 minutes approx on each occasion. Such bombs were craters shelled throughout day intermittently. 2 O.R. wounded on ration party.	

Army Form C. 2118.

WAR DIARY
or
INTELLIGENCE SUMMARY.
(Erase heading not required.)

Place	Date	Hour	Summary of Events and Information	Remarks and references to Appendices
	Aug 30		Wind S.W. Cloudy, with intervals of bright sunshine. Visibility fair. WESTHOEK RIDGE bombarded with 4.2" and 5.9" intermittently throughout daylight. 3 E.A. flew low over WESTHOEK at 6.30 am. Were engaged by M.G. from J.I.C.2.2. Rounds fired 350. Sent flash cartridges at S.A.A. dump at J.I.6.2.2.	
	31		Wind S.W. 4 E.A. flying low on our lines to westward of WESTHOEK at dawn. Fired on by M.G. from J.I.C.90.20. Rounds fired 500. Enemy barrage opened on WESTHOEK RIDGE from 8.0 pm to 11.0 pm. No inf. Casualties. Infantry supported a few rounds 30000 rounds sent to dump at J.I.6.B0.00.	

O.C. 162 M.G. Coy.

guns & equipment will proceed to the forward area by limber under arrangements made by O.C. Coy concerned. Lorries will wait at the BRASSERIE & convey the personnel of the 194 M.G. Coy to their transport lines at PIEBROUCH FARM (R.27.a.30.90.)

4) All movements forward of the BRASSERIE will be by sections.

5) O.C. 124 M.G. Coy is notified that he is responsible for providing 1 barrage battery in addition to the defensive guns of the left sector.

6) On the relief being completed A, C & D batteries will be responsible for the barrage under the executive orders of the D.M.G.O. pending further orders & arrangements. New barrage tables will be issued for these batteries to-morrow 5th inst.

7) Completion of relief will be announced personally to D.M.G.O by O.C relieved coys.

8) ACKNOWLEDGE.

W H Davis
Major D.M.G.O

D.M.G.O/4.1/73.　　　　　　　　　　4/8/17

From/
    D.M.G.O.
      41st Division.

To
    O.C. 142 M.G. Coy
     " 194   "
     " 238   "
     " 124   "

Ref: attached copy of 41st Divl. Order No 149

Please act. (ref: para: 2)

1) Arrangements made between O's C. 194 M.G. Coy & 238 M.G. Coy for the relief of 'C' & 'D' Batteries will hold good. Guides from these Batteries will be at Norfolk Bridge at I.33.d.3.5. at 1.pm.

2) 142 M.G. Coy will vacate their barrage positions commencing at 1 pm, & proceed to their Transport lines under arrangements to be made by O.C. Coys concerned.

3) Lorries will be placed at the disposal of the 238 Coy & will convey the personnel of the Coy to the BRASSERIE (N.6.a.15.15)

Secret.

Copy of 41st Division Order No. 149.

4 August 1917

1. The Machine Gun Companies 47th & 23rd Division, at present forming part of the Machine Gun Barrage covering 41st Division front, will return to the command of their respective Divisions from 5th inst, & will rejoin their Divisions on that date, under arrangements to be made by Divisional Machine Gun Officer.
Q will arrange for transport.

2. The 238 Machine Gun Coy will move up to the Brigade Sector North of the CANAL, & take over two of the barrage batteries of the Machine Gun Coys of the 23rd & 47th Divisional Companies.
Relief will take place at 2 p.m. on 5th inst under arrangements to be made by Divisional Machine Gun Officer. Q will arrange transport.

3. On the same date (August 5th) 141st Infantry Brigade will withdraw to the 47th Division area under orders of G.O.C. 47th Division.

4. Acknowledge.

(signed) R. G. Parker
Lt. Colonel G.S.

Issued to Signals 10. a.m.

Army Form C. 2118.

142nd M.G.Coy

Vol 22

WAR DIARY
INTELLIGENCE SUMMARY.
(Erase heading not required.)

Place	Date	Hour	Summary of Events and Information	Remarks and references to Appendices
	Sept 1.		Disposition 10 guns in defensive position in forward area on WESTHOEK RIDGE. 4 guns at J.1.c.20.20 in Barrage position. Weather clear during day. Rain at night. Enemy aircraft engaged 0.30 a.m. no direct result. 3 sections relieved during night by 3 section of 126 Company 42nd Division. 9 other ranks wounded during relief. Relieved sections returned to MONTREAL CAMP near OUDERDOM.	
	Sept 2.		Weather Bright. 3 sections moved from MONTREAL CAMP to SCOTTISH LINES Camp at G.23.6.20.20. (Belgium 28 NW 1/20,000.) Remaining guns relieved by 74th Company, 23rd Division; and returned to SCOTTISH LINES CAMP. Camp shelled by Enemy (approx) H.V. gun. No damage done.	
	Sept 3.		Wet. Snell weather clear. Kit inspection and interior economy. Camp shelled by H.V. gun. 6 in. and was temporarily evacuated. No damage done.	
	Sept 4.		Wind South, weather warm & bright. Enemy aircraft very active on both areas throughout night. Company training and interior economy.	
	Sept 5.		Wind S.E. Bright, clear. Company left SCOTTISH LINES for STEENVOORDE area. Left camp 9.50 a.m. arrived billets in STEENVOORDE – WINIZEELE ROAD J.21.a.90.15 (sheet 27) at 2.45 p.m.	
	Sept 6		Wind S.E. Hot, thundery some rain. Company training.	

WAR DIARY
or
INTELLIGENCE SUMMARY.

(Erase heading not required.)

Army Form C. 2118.

Instructions regarding War Diaries and Intelligence Summaries are contained in F. S. Regs., Part II. and the Staff Manual respectively. Title pages will be prepared in manuscript.

Place	Date	Hour	Summary of Events and Information	Remarks and references to Appendices
	Sept 7		Wind S.E. Warm and bright. Company training. 2 OR reported for duty from base.	
	Sept 8		Wind S.E. Company training.	
	Sept 9		Weather warm and clear. Company parades with 22nd London for Church Parade.	
	Sept 10		Wind E. Weather colder. Company moved by busses from STEENVOORDE area to PIONEER camp area (N. of DICKEBUSCH) as divisional reserve. Transport moved by road, was shelled in the vicinity of OUDERDOM. Billets were taken over from the 75th Company.	
	Sept 11		Wind N.E. Weather clear and hot. Lumber cleaning and kit inspection. Anti aircraft mountings improvised and H guns mounted. A few shells fell in vicinity of house lines; no damage was done.	
	Sept 12		Weather unchanged. Horse lines moved to Camp at H.27.b.6.7. Company training.	
	Sept 13		Weather unchanged. Company training. Some shelling in vicinity of camp during night. No damage done.	
	Sept 14		Wind N. Some rain during night, few showers by day. Company training. Company bathed during morning at HALIFAX BATHS on VLAMERTINGHE—OUDERDOM ROAD.	
	Sept 15		Wind N.W. Enemy aircraft engaged about 12.15 p.m. 800 rounds fired, no observed result. Tracer bullets showed the direction of fire very fair.	

Army Form C. 2118.

WAR DIARY
or
INTELLIGENCE SUMMARY.
(Erase heading not required.)

Instructions regarding War Diaries and Intelligence Summaries are contained in F. S. Regs., Part II. and the Staff Manual respectively. Title pages will be prepared in manuscript.

Place	Date	Hour	Summary of Events and Information	Remarks and references to Appendices
	Sept 16		Wind NW. Weather bright + clear. Company leaves CANAL RESERVE CAMP at 7.50 and marches to DALLINGTON CAMP near REMY SIDING. Arrived at REMY SIDING 12.30 pm.	
	Sept 17		Wind N. Company training + routine inspections.	
	Sept 18		Wind E. Some showers, especially at mid day. Company paraded by march route to ST. SYLVESTRE CAPPEL. Arrived 1 pm.	
	Sept 19 + 20		Weather bright + clear. Company training and pay parade.	
	Sept 21		Wind S.E. Weather warm + clear. Company paraded to CASSEL STATION by march route and entrained at 4.30 pm for MAROEUIL. Arrived 11.30 pm and proceeded to billets in MAROEUIL.	
	Sept 22		Wind S.E. Weather hot + clean. Company moved to billets in ANZIN. Advance party reconnoitred line.	
	Sept 23		Wind E. Weather hot + clear. Company relieved 16 guns 190th Company 63rd (R.N.) Division in OPPY SECTOR.	
	Sept 24		Wind S.E. Weather hot + clear. Line very quiet. 6,000 rds fired during night on LINK MAZE and LAMBERT ALLEY. (Reference OPPY SIG NW 2)	
	Sept 25		Wind E. MARINE Trench shelled with 4.25 between 2 pm and 3 pm. 6,000 rds fired during night at C3 c 50.80 C2 b a H5.05 C2 0 c 55.20 (Hq B's harbour Dugouts)	

Army Form C. 2118.

WAR DIARY
or
INTELLIGENCE SUMMARY.
(Erase heading not required.)

Place	Date	Hour	Summary of Events and Information	Remarks and references to Appendices
	Sept 26		Wind E. Weather bright and clear. Enemy Artillery slightly more active especially on vicinity of Light Railway and TYNE ALLEY. 4,250 rds fired during night on OPPY-NEUVIREUIL ROAD C7.C10.10 and CRUMB TRENCH (Ref FOOTHILLS 25000)	
	Sept 27		Wind 6. Weather fine and clear. Enemy Aircraft active between 3.30 pm and 5 pm. During night 2,000 rds fired at CRUMB TRENCH 2,000 at LAMBERT ALLEY, 1,000 at tracks leading to CHERAP TRENCH	
	Sept 28		Wind E. Weather clear. During night several "Pineapple" bombs fired on front line near BRADFORD ALLEY. Four casualties to Infantry. 4000 rds fired on OPPY support trench OPPY-NEUVIREUIL ROAD and C26 a 4.5.0.5	
	Sept 29		Wind E. Weather clear and bright. Considerable number of "Pineapple" Bombs on front line between 6.30 pm and 7.30 pm and about midnight. 4,750 rds fired at OPPY SUPPORT, CRUMB TRENCH and CAVRELLE SUPPORT	

Army Form C. 2118.

WAR DIARY
or
INTELLIGENCE SUMMARY.
(Erase heading not required.)

Instructions regarding War Diaries and Intelligence Summaries are contained in F. S. Regs., Part II. and the Staff Manual respectively. Title pages will be prepared in manuscript.

Place	Date	Hour	Summary of Events and Information	Remarks and references to Appendices
	Sept 30		Wind E. Misty until 8.30 am. Clear remainder of day. Enemy aircraft active during morning otherwise no activity. 6.00 no fire on OPPY ROAD and CRUMP TRENCH. No casualties have been sustained in this sector between Sept 23rd and Sept 30th. Dispositions were one section in front system, 2 sections in support system, 1 in reserve line.	B.R. White Capt.

2353 Wt. W2544/1454 700,000 5/15 D. D. & L. A.D.S.S.Forms/C. 2118.

Army Form C. 2118.

142nd M.G. Coy
Vol 2

WAR DIARY
or
INTELLIGENCE SUMMARY.
(Erase heading not required.)

Place	Date	Hour	Summary of Events and Information	Remarks and references to Appendices
	Oct 1		Wind E. Company in left sub sector of GAVRELLE - OPPY Sector. Disposition 3 sections in front system and one in reserve line. Enemy activity below normal. 5000 rounds fired on tracks between OPPY and GAVRELLE	
	2		Wind 6. Weather clear. Enemy activity normal. Inter-section reliefs carried out. 2000 rds fired on GAVRELLE SUPPORT trench. 2250 rds fired on roads & tracks	
	3		Wind S.E. Some rain and cloudy. 3500 rds fired on tracks in vicinity of OPPY	
	4		Wind E. Weather clear. Some shelling on left of Sector during morning. No damage done. 5,000 rds fired during night on track from MAVILLE FARM to front line. In co-operation with Artillery, no information from Prisoners indicated Battalion relief.	
	5		Wind S.E. Weather clear. Enemy very quiet. 2040 rds fired on MAVILLE FARM track. 2,000 rds fired on GAVRELLE ROAD	
	6		Wind SE. Weather wet & cloudy. Enemy activity nil. 2000 rds fired on tracks near LINK MAZE. 2000 rds fired OPPY - NEUVIREUIL ROAD. Inter section relief carried out.	
	7		Wind E. Cloudy during morning. Rain in afternoon and evening. 2 guns withdrawn from	

Army Form C. 2118.

WAR DIARY
or
INTELLIGENCE SUMMARY.
(Erase heading not required.)

Instructions regarding War Diaries and Intelligence Summaries are contained in F.S. Regs., Part II. and the Staff Manual respectively. Title pages will be prepared in manuscript.

Place	Date	Hour	Summary of Events and Information	Remarks and references to Appendices
	8		Front line to Support trench. 2000 rds fired on MAUVILLE FARM track 2500 rds on track east of WINDMILL MAIZE. Wind E. Intermittent rain throughout day and night. Enemy activity nil	
	9		2500 rds fired on rondo and tracks S of OPPY. 2000 rds fired on MAUVILLE FARM track. Wind N.E. Weather wet and stormy	
	10		2000 rds fired on tracks EAST of WINDMILL MAIZE Wind E. Rain during morning - clear in afternoon. Company relieved by 140 M.G.C.y and returned to Reserve Billets at ANZIN-ST-AUBIN. During this period on the line the Company had no casualties	
	11		Wind N.E. Intermittent rain throughout day. Kit Inspections and Interior Economy	
	12		Wind E. Weather cloudy - no rain. Baths and Company training	
	13		Wind E. Weather clear. Company training.	
	14/15		Wind E. Weather clear. Interior Economy.	
	16		Wind E. Weather clear and bright. Company training	
	17		Wind N.E. Weather clear. Company training	
	18		Wind. Weather clear. Company relieved 141 Machine Gun Coy in GAVREILLE	FRANC 51° NW 1/20,000

WAR DIARY
or
INTELLIGENCE SUMMARY.
(Erase heading not required.)

Army Form C. 2118.

Place	Date	Hour	Summary of Events and Information	Remarks and references to Appendices
	19		SECTOR. Relief complete 1.45 p.m. Dispositions Front system 9 guns Red line 6 guns, 1 gun mobile reserve at Company Headquarters. 3000 rds fired from B 29 & 30.45 at enemy tracks. Wind SE. Weather dull. Enemy guns quiet during day but Machine gun active at night. 3000 rds fired from B.29 & 30.45 at road junction B 36 a 00.80 and WINDMILL MAIZE. Construction of shelters for new positions at C 19 c 05.12 commenced	
	20		Wind SE. Weather fine. Hostile artillery normal. 3,000 rds fired from B 29 & 30.45 on area around C 26 central and C 20 a 50.25.	
	21		Wind W. Hostile artillery below normal. The railway gun in D.9.c was active, firing on back areas. 3000 rds fired from B 29 & 30.45 on C 26 c 6.7 and C 26 a 7.9	
	22		Wind SW. Hostile artillery almost inactive on our front. 3000 rds fired from B 29 & 30.45 on road at C 26 a 6.7. and back C 20.c 50.85	
	23		Wind W. Hostile artillery inactive during the day, but objective shelling of TOWY ALLEY and GAVRELLE in retaliation for fire on our immediate right. 3000 rds fired from B 29 & 30.45 on area about C 26 central and back C 20. C. 50.85	
	24		Wind NW. From 2.30 pm to 4.30 pm and again at 9.30 pm barrages were put down on our	

Army Form C. 2118.

WAR DIARY
or
INTELLIGENCE SUMMARY.
(Erase heading not required.)

Place	Date	Hour	Summary of Events and Information	Remarks and references to Appendices.
	25		Front + Support lines in B25 and I1; shells were mostly 10.5 percussion. 3,000 rds fired B29 & B30.45 on hook at C26 c 53.85 and rest at C26 a 70.90. Wind N.W. Hostile artillery quiet. 3000 rds fired from B29 & B30.45 on area round C26 c7 and C26 central.	
	26		Wind NW. Enemy artillery activity normal. 3000 rds fire from B29 & B30.45 at road C26 a 0.8. and C25 & C8.8. Intersection. relief carried out.	
	27		Wind N.W. Between 9 am and 10 am. —5. B27 & and B28 a shelled by 5.9. During the afternoon GAUR ETUL and front system were shelled. 3000 rds fired from B29 & B30.45 on C26 central and C26 c 6.7.	
	28		Wind W. BAILEUL heavily shelled until 4.2 during the afternoon, thorough enemy activity normal. 3000 rds fire from B29 & B30.45 on C20 c 50.85 and C26 central. During the night changed to easterly direction for a short while.	
	29		Wind S.W. Enemy artillery activity above normal especially on CHICO + WILLIE trenches. 3000 rds fired from B29 & B30.45 on the WINDMILL HAZE and C26 a 0.2.	
	30		Wind S.W. Enemy artillery activity slightly above normal, especially on the front WILLIE TRENCH and CHICO TRENCH. 3000 rds fired from B29 & B30.45 on	

Army Form C. 2118.

WAR DIARY
or
INTELLIGENCE SUMMARY.
(Erase heading not required.)

Place	Date	Hour	Summary of Events and Information	Remarks and references to Appendices
	31st		C26 a 7.9 and C26 a.6.7. Wind W. Enemy artillery activity slightly above normal, especially on front CHICO and WILLIE trenches. At 11.30 a.m. 600 rds fired on enemy support lines whilst reconnaissance was being carried out by low-flying aeroplane. During the night 1500 rds fired on gunpits in enemy wire, opposite WILLIE and CHICO trenches, 3000 rds fired from B29 & 20.45; on C26 central and C20 c 50.55.	[signature]

B.F. Davies/ Capt.
O.C. 162 Siege Coy.

142nd Inf Bde

Herewith Original War Diary
for November, please

G W Anstin
Lieut
for Capt
Commdg
142 M.G. Coy

142nd
MACHINE GUN
COMPANY.
No. A90
Date 2. 12. 17.

WAR DIARY or INTELLIGENCE SUMMARY

Army Form C. 2118.

142nd M.G. Coy.
Vol 24

Place	Date	Hour	Summary of Events and Information	Remarks and references to Appendices
GAVRELLE SECTOR	Nov 1st		Wind S.W. Company in GAVRELLE SECTOR. Dispositions: 3 guns in front system; 6 guns in 2nd line; 6 guns in Reserve line; 1 gun in Reserve at Coy HQ. Hostile artillery above normal; enemy retaliating for our wire-cutting east of GAVRELLE, 3,000 rounds fired on enemy wire (cut by our heavy artillery) in C25d.; 3,000 rounds fired on road in C25d and C26a.	REF MAP 51B.S.E.
	2		Wind S.W. Hostile artillery quiet during morning; from 10.pm to 11.pm, enemy shelled front system and TOMMY ALLEY with 4HV. and 4.9 Howitzers. 2,000 rounds fired on enemy wire in C25d.; 3,000 rds fired at junction of road and road C25 & C18.	
	3		Wind S., changing in the afternoon to S.E. Enemy activity normal. In addition to normal night firing 3000 rds were fired on wire of GAVRELLE TRENCH front S.E. Weather dull and mild. Day quiet off 11.30 pm a great air	
	4		carried out by 23rd and 248 Batts London Regt. 12 guns of the Company were employed in firing barrage. Fire was maintained for approx for 60 minutes after ZERO and intermittently from zero plus 60 to ZERO plus 90 55,000 rds fired during operations. No casualties to personnel or damage to guns. 18 prisoners 2 machine guns and 2 trench mortars were	

WAR DIARY
or
INTELLIGENCE SUMMARY

Army Form C. 2118.

Place	Date	Hour	Summary of Events and Information	Remarks and references to Appendices
	5		captured in raid. Wind S.S.E. Weather misty and dull. Company relieved by 140 Machine Gun Coy in GAVRELLE SECTOR and proceeded in reserve at ANZIN. Relief complete at 2.30 p.m. Company in billets at 6.45 p.m.	
	6		Wind W. Weather dull. Baths, Interior Economy and Pay Parade. 9th C.P.W.R.E. explosion Establishment present at D.P.S.E.	
	7		Wind N.W. Weather wet. School of Instruction in billets	
	8		Wind N.W. Weather wet. Bull filling Lebanon and D.Hyppogen	
	9		Wind W. Weather showery throughout day. Company=Route March.	
	10		Wind W. Weather showery. Company training including Lebanon & D.Hyppogen	
	11		Wind N. Weather clear. Company Church Parade. Football in afternoon in Divisional League.	
	12		Wind S. Weather misty but no rain. Company training and preparations for going in the line	
	13		Wind W. Weather fine but misty. The Company takes over Bochine	

Army Form C. 2118.

WAR DIARY
or
INTELLIGENCE SUMMARY.
(Erase heading not required.)

Instructions regarding War Diaries and Intelligence Summaries are contained in F. S. Regs., Part II. and the Staff Manual respectively. Title pages will be prepared in manuscript.

Place	Date	Hour	Summary of Events and Information	Remarks and references to Appendices
	14		Gun defence of Divisional front on the OPPY - GAVRELLE sector. New Wireless Post Scheme comes into force to which tune is held by seven posts - the gaps being expect whenever possible by direct machine Gun fire. 11 guns at 143 Bty employed in covering gaps between posts. 5 guns in Reserve Line and 8 guns at 140 Bty in barrage positions. Enemy very quiet. Relief complete by 5 p.m. Light firing - 1000 rounds fired on tracks. Wind W. Weather misty. Normal. Enemy activity nil. Night firing - 5000 rds fired on enemy tracks. Wind S.W. Weather misty.	
	15		Very little activity on divisional front during morning. During the afternoon left sector heavily shelled - little damage done.	
		7.30pm	The Division on right (61st Division) carried out a raid. Some retaliation on GAVRELLE and the vicinity of the WINDMILL 5000 rds fired on GAVRELLE - FRESNES road. Wind E. Weather clear. Enemy activity normal. 3000 rds fired on	
	16		tracks west of MAUVILLE FARM. 3000 on NEUVIREUIL-OPPY road	

WAR DIARY
or
INTELLIGENCE SUMMARY.
(Erase heading not required.)

Army Form C. 2118.

Place	Date	Hour	Summary of Events and Information	Remarks and references to Appendices
	17		Wind N.E. Weather mild. Enemy activity below normal. 6,000 rds fired on tracks between WINDMILL and OPPY VILLAGE	
	18		Wind N.E. Weather dull. Company relieved on Divisional front by 2nd I.L.C.H. Relief complete by 4.30pm. Company proceeded into reserve at ECURIE WOOD. During this tour of duty in the trenches the Company suffered no casualties. 5 men reported sick.	
	19		Wind W. Some rain. Interior economy.	
	20		Wind N.W. Weather wet. Company inspection and training. to O.R.D. Y. PATON left to join 202 I.L.C.H (66th Division) on promotion to Warrant Officer (Class II)	
	21		Wind W. Rain throughout day. Company moved to MONT ST ELOY at 10 am and arrived 1pm.	
	22		Wind N.W. Weather cloudy - no rain. Company moved to fields in BERNEVILLE starting at 9.55 am and arriving 2 pm.	
	23		Wind N. Company inspection. Interior economy.	
	24		Wind N.W. Cold but little rain. Company moved at 8 am and arrived at	

WAR DIARY
or
INTELLIGENCE SUMMARY.

(Erase heading not required.)

Army Form C. 2118.

Place	Date	Hour	Summary of Events and Information	Remarks and references to Appendices
	25		GOMIECOURT at 2.30 pm. Billetted in tents and bivouacs. Wind S.W. Day cold - some sleet. Company moved off at 1 pm arrived in Camp at BARASTRE at 8 pm. March very slow, considerable congestion N.W. of BAPAUME. B.Q.M.S. PERRINS joined Company for duties.	
	26		Wind N.W. Weather very cold. 10 a.m. Interior economy.	
	27		Wind W. The Company moved to BEAUMETZ-LES-CAMBRAI arriving in billets at 7.30 pm.	
	28		Wind S.W. Interior Economy.	
	29		Wind N.W. The Company moved at 5.30 pm into Brigade Divisional Reserve in Hindenburg Line in K.15.d.	
	30		Wind N.W. Company moved by sections to support of 2nd Division. C and D sections moved by sections to support of 2nd Division positions in KANGAROO ALLEY in E.28.c. E.27.d. at 11 a.m. At night C and D Sections remained in positions. A Section moved to Hindenburg Support in K.10.d. B Section moved back to Hindenburg Line in K.15.d. One other ranks killed, two other ranks wounded and one other rank (att) wounded - shellshock.	[signature] [signature] 147 M.A. Coy

Army Form C. 2118.

142 M G Coy
25

WAR DIARY
or
INTELLIGENCE SUMMARY.
(Erase heading not required.)

Place	Date	Hour	Summary of Events and Information	Remarks and references to Appendices
	Dec 1		Wind N.W. Some rain mizzling towards evening. Company deepened with 2 sections in outpost of 2nd Division in KANGAROO ALLEY South of BAPAUME - CAMBRAI ROAD. 1 Section in reserve in HINDENBURG LINE, 1 Section in L.I.a covering right flank of Division. At 8.00 pm Company ordered to relieve 141st M G Coy in BOURLON WOOD. No guides. Company arrived BOURLON WOOD 5.30 a.m. on and took over 12 positions in wood. Two casualties (wounded) occurred going in and were shortly after by 1 killed 6 wounded, 2 shell shock. Shelling heavy in wood but no further casualties. Wind E. Weather clear.	BOURLON 57c N.E.2
	2			
	3		Wind E. Cold and frosty. Enemy artillery active and wood shelled heavily in morning and evening. At 9.00 pm gas shell bombardment of wood started and lasted until 2.00 am. No casualties. A out section of 142 M G Coy took over 2 guns of 255 M G Coy on right of front.	
	4		Wind E. Cold and frosty. Enemy shelled very heavily at dawn. 2 killed and 3 wounded in "C" Section. Day quiet. At 3.30 am all M.G. ordered to 5th Bde M G Cos. Were told of intention to evacuate BOURLON WOOD silent and withdrawn to vicinity of HINDENBURG SUPPORT LINE. This was done by 3.00 am on Dec 5th B Section left with outpost line.	
	5		Wind E. Cold and frosty. Company take up position 1 Section in HINDENBURG SUPPORT LINE. Remainder in HINDENBURG LINE. Day quiet.	

WAR DIARY or INTELLIGENCE SUMMARY

Army Form C. 2118.

Place	Date	Hour	Summary of Events and Information	Remarks and references to Appendices
NOEUVRES 1/20000	Dec 6		Wind N.W. Weather fine. At dusk A & C Sections moved forward from positions in Hindenburg Line to Outposts as follows :— "B" Sub-Section under Lt. Pitt to K.4.d.1.5. "A" Sub-Section under 2/Lt Ignis to K.4.a.2.0. 2C Section under Lt. Pakenham to K.11.a.2.7. During the morning "B" Section 2/C Chambers in Post in K.6.fr were attacked by large force of the enemy. A copy of report of the action of "B" Section is attached to the Original War Diary. The men of this Section who were surrounded made their way to Bn H.Q. in Hindenburg Line. During night Bn H.Q. were moved to K.10.c.7.4.	
	7		Wind E. Weather cold but fine. The post in K.4.a.2.0. received attention during day from enemy snipers and rifle grenades. The post in K.11.a.2.7 was shelled intermittently throughout day with 4.2" 5.0" & 1" trench guns but without serious damage. Otherwise the shelling was less heavy than the preceding few days. During day 3000 rds fired from K.4.a on enemy movements.	
	8		Wind E. Weather fine. Enemy artillery active during day.	
	9		Wind E. Weather cold and frosty. Little rain in afternoon. The Post in K.4.d.2.5. (occupied by 2/37 Bn London Regiment and "A" Sub-Section under	

WAR DIARY or INTELLIGENCE SUMMARY

Army Form C. 2118.

(Erase heading not required.)

Place	Date	Hour	Summary of Events and Information	Remarks and references to Appendices
			(2 Pdr) was attacked shortly after dawn. Both guns opened fire on the enemy but were temporarily outflanked. One gun was blown up by an enemy shell and the N°1 (Cpl. Faulkner) killed. The other gun was put out of action to prevent it falling into enemy hands. The losses of the sub-section during this action were - killed 1 O.R., wounded & missing 1 O.R., wounded 1 O.R. (Lieut Pitt) & missing 3 O.R. The enemy shelled Hughes Dunkirk and Harrincourt road heavily. During the action in post K.4.a.2.5 approximately 1500 rds were fired. 2,000 rds. were fired during night on roads in Trincourt. "A" Sub.Section under 99th Lorrie evacuated the post at K.4.a. 2.0 during night and arrived at K.U.a.2.7. and withdrew to 6th H.Q. about 2.00 am on Dec 10th. "C" Section also evacuated post at K.U.a.2.7. and withdrew to 6th HQ. arriving about 6am on Dec 10th. Enemy	MOEUVRE 5 1/20,000
	Dec 10		Wind N.W. Weather fine. "D" Section withdrew to Dunkirk road in K.9.c. artillery activity greatly decreased. During the day the Depot and transport lines S. of Harrincourt wood were bombed and shelled. No casualties to animals at L.G. Personnel. 14 O.R. reinforcements reported at Depot	
	11		Wind N.W. Rain during morning. Enemy quiet. 6th HA. moved to 255.M.9.6th for night at K. 15. d. 2.2. Enemy A/Gs did usual night firing on Harrincourt road. 500 rds fired on enemy aircraft from K.15c. about 2.15 am.	
	12		Wind N.W. Weather fine. Day quiet. "D"Section relieved by 255 M.G.Cy and withdrew to K.16. c.18. to join 4 guns of "C" Section --- Dispositions now are 2 batteries of 8 guns each ---	

WAR DIARY
or
INTELLIGENCE SUMMARY.

Army Form C. 2118.

Place	Date	Hour	Summary of Events and Information	Remarks and references to Appendices
MOEUVRES			No 2 Battery at K.16.c.1.9. A & D Sections	
			No 4 Battery at K.22.t. B & D Sections	1/20,000
			10th HQ move to K.21.a.y.2.	
	Dec 13		Wind N.W. Weather clear. Enemy activity considerably lessened.	
			During night 20,000 rounds were fired on enemy Junction, roads, and tracks in K.4.a. K.5.c. K.11.a. K.11.t. K.12.c. K.12.a. firing commencing 6.30pm and ceasing 7 am Dec 14th.	
	14		Wind N. Weather bright and clear. Enemy activity practically nil.	
			19,500 rds fired from positions on Roads & Tracks in K.5.c. K.4.a. K.11.a. and t. K.12.c. and a. firing continued from dusk until dawn.	
	15		Wind N. Weather very clear & bright. Enemy aeroplanes active during morning. 6 E.A. flying low over forward positions between 6.50 am and 7.30 am. fired on by Nos 2 and No 4. Batteries but no result observed. Enemy artillery fairly active taking advantage of the exceptionally clear day registered on numerous targets but otherwise enemy activity was small. The usual harrassing fire on enemy roads and tracks was continued 24000 rounds being fired	
	16		Wind N.W. Weather bright. Enemy very quiet. A & B Sections Journey No 2 Battery were relieved by guns of the 140 L. Bty and proceeded to billets at NEUVILLE	

Army Form C. 2118.

WAR DIARY
or
INTELLIGENCE SUMMARY.
(Erase heading not required.)

Instructions regarding War Diaries and Intelligence Summaries are contained in F.S. Regs., Part II. and the Staff Manual respectively. Title pages will be prepared in manuscript.

Place	Date	Hour	Summary of Events and Information	Remarks and references to Appendices
			arriving at 8.00 a.m 17th (?) 3 Divisions leaving 119 & Battery were relieved 3 & 4 guns of 141 L.O.By. and proceeded to VILLE at BERTINCOURT arriving at 6 a.m. on December 17th. During the night no news of us was obtained.	FRANCE 5/8 1/40000
Dec 17			Major N.E. & D Divisions proceeded by Motor Lorries in a decoration to VILLE at BRESLE arriving in VILLE about 8 p.m.	LENS 11 1/40000
	18		Major N.E. & B Divisions entrained at VELU and detrained at ALBERT and found comrades & Company at BRESLE about 9.30 p.m.	AMIENS.17 1/40000
	19		Wind N.W. Weather cold and frosty. Ordinary routine inspection. During the period 17th Dec 18th the Brigade met with the Company suffered casualties as follows, Killed 1 Officer wounded and missing (not November 9) and 1 Officer wounded (2nd Lut D) killed 5 O.R. wounded missing 2 O.R. Missing 1 O.R. 14 O.R. reinforcement joined from the 25 Batt and continuants	
			were evacuated sick	
	20		Wind R.E Weather cold. Slight snow storm during morning. Company training.	
	21		Wind N.E Weather cold and windy. Company inspection. Gases for A.H.Q. Lecture Pol: Brigade.	
	22		Wind N.E. Weather cold and misty. Interior economy. Continued instructions	
	23		Wind N.E. Weather cold. Intense Squatter Practice during morning	

WAR DIARY
or
INTELLIGENCE SUMMARY.

Army Form C. 2118.

(Erase heading not required.)

Place	Date	Hour	Summary of Events and Information	Remarks and references to Appendices
Doullens			March to Doullens	AMIENS 1/100,000
	26		Weather fair & cold. Company Parade at 10.45. Company Drill.	
	27		NE. Horseman Training	
	28		NE. Weather cold and foggy. Slight snowstorm during morning. Usual day.	
	29		NE. Weather frosty. Company Training	
	30		NE. Frosty and cold. Showers during and periods of Instruction.	
	30		NE. Weather frosty. Both suspension during morning. Usual 3pm after	57° 40000
			3 hours notice the Company had Q.L. Duty moved from Wills at BRESLE	
			and marched to ALBERT when the transport and guns limbers returned.	
			The transport, supply & the road. The party were further divided, the night was	
			bitterly cold. ROCQUIGNY at about 6pm. On the	
			and after breakfast marched to limits at ETRICOURT arriving about 3 am	
			The transport arrived about 10pm	

Robert ____
for Capt
O/C 14th M.G. Coy.

Report on action of "B" Section 142 M.G.C.'s on December 4th 5th and 6th when operating with 140 Inf Bde to cover withdrawal from the BOURLON Salient

This Report has been compiled partly from the statements of men of "B" Section 142 M.G.C. and partly from the statement of Sgt Mankthorpe the senior surviving N.C.O. of the two Companies of the 15th Bn London Regiment

Ref Maps BOURLON 1/10,000
MOEUVRES 1/20,000

On the afternoon of Decr 4th orders were received that the Section of 142 M.G.C. under Lt Chambers in reserve at K.6.b.50.60. was to be attached to the 140 Inf Bde to assist in covering the withdrawal of the 47th Div. from the Bourlon wood salient to the vicinity of Hindenburg Support Line

The strength of this Section was 1 off. and 27 O.R.

Their orders were to select positions in the vicinity of the gun pits in K.6.b. where an outpost was to be found of 2 coys of 15th Bn from which the ridge E of Graincourt could be covered.   These positions were selected by 2/Lt Chambers after consultation with Major Waine who was in command of the Outpost and were duly occupied shortly after midnight of the 4/5 Dec.

The night of the 4/5 was uneventful but about noon on the 5th Dec small parties of the enemy were seen in the direction of ANNEUX and towards 4pm a few of the enemy were seen to enter Graincourt. These patrols were sniped at by the Outpost.

From time to time during the night of 5/6 further small bodies of the enemy approached the Outpost from E and N but disappeared after being fired on by Lewis and machine guns.   It was reported early on the 6th that enemy patrols had been seen on the southern and western outskirts of Graincourt.

During the morning of the 6th Dec. the enemy exposed themselves in larger numbers E of Graincourt and were fired on from time to time by Machine Guns and driven to cover.   On one of these occasions 1 of the 4 Vickers guns was damaged and apparently could not be repaired. A message was sent by runner asking for it to be replaced, but D.O.C. 110 Inf Bde considered this to be inadvisable.   Later in the day 2/Lt Chambers ordered this gun to be completely destroyed as there appeared to be a possibility of its falling into enemy hands.

About 10 am it was reported that enemy patrols moving out from Raincourt had established themselves in the rear of the left flank of the position and a stand to was accordingly ordered.

At about 3.30 p.m. a large force of the enemy appeared over the Ridge in F.25. and L.1.a. and advanced obliquely across the front of the Outpost in a southwesterly direction. The strength of this force is variously estimated but the average would appear to be about 800. At this time also enemy artillery put down a somewhat ragged barrage on the right of the Outpost in about L.1. central and a heavy machine gun fire was opened against the post and Sunken Road in K.6.A.

Rapid fire was promptly opened against this force by the Garrison of the post and very heavy casualties were seen to be inflicted and considerable confusion caused.

The Vickers gun on the extreme right flank was in position at approximately L.1.a.30.20 in a Trench with men from the Sherwood Foresters.   This gun had fired some 4 or 5 belt, when it received orders from an Officer of the Sherwoods to withdraw with the infantry. The No 1 on this gun Cpl Baxter finished the belt already in the gun and loaded in a new belt. He and the No 2 (L/Cpl Moore) then dismounted the gun, shouted to the spare numbers to run for it and set out after the Sherwoods carrying the gun, tripod and a spare belt of ammunition. They moved South across the Sunken Road but after proceeding for about 400 yards Cpl Baxter, seeing a large body of the enemy following stopped with L/Cpl Moore mounted the gun and opened fire. By this time they had become separated by some considerable distance from the remainder of the withdrawing force and nothing further is known of them. They are accordingly reported missing.

    The above account was furnished by Pte Hallet and corroborated by Ptes Bleaver and Wood who formed the other members of the team.

    The remaining 2 Vickers guns were on the left flank under the control of Pte Chambers who was wounded in the thigh shortly after 3.30 p.m. but remained at his post. Both guns fired until their ammunition was almost exhausted and the Companies of the 16th B"" commenced to withdraw. It was then found

5

that parties of the enemy had completely outflanked the position and the only line of retreat was in a South Easterly direction turning later South West towards FLESQUERS

The team of the gun that had been destroyed were acting as Riflemen and withdrew with the 15th Bn with the exception of Pte Saunders who had been detailed to assist with one of the guns that under L/Cpl Buckley the other gun being under Cpl Brunswick. Seeing the situation 2/Lt Chambers ordered both guns to withdraw and advised moving Eastwards along the Sunken Road in K.6.B. to avoid the encircling patrols of the enemy. The only serious casualties among the Machine Gunners up to this time were Lt Chambers hit in the thigh, and Pte McCullock with a bullet wound in the side. Of these 2 Pte McCullock was already in the Trench connecting the gun pits and could not be moved. 2/Lt Chambers was also unable to walk and while the gun teams were getting away Sgt Butler his Section Sergeant remained behind to help him into a dug-out, and as no further report has been received of 2/Lt Chambers, Sgt Butler or Pte McCullock they are believed to have fallen into the hands of the enemy

Meanwhile the withdrawing troops found themselves hard pressed by a party of the enemy coming from the direction of Raincourt and as they were unable to move fast carrying loads all the surplus gear was dropped except the 2 guns which they took turns in carrying.

The Companies of the 15th appear to have withdrawn almost due West and running into a party of the enemy fought their way through and brought back a few prisoners.

The 2 gun teams, however, following 2/Lt Chambers advice started off Eastwards along the Sunken road in K.6.b. and after about 500 yards turned off to the right across Country. At this point the party got split up and mixed with some infantry retiring at the double. Cpl Penwarwick who was carrying his gun at this time was last seen here, and has not since been heard of. He is accordingly reported missing.

L/Cpl Buckley and his team fared better and 4 of them succeeded in keeping together until they reached Sunken Road which later proved to be that running from Raincourt to Flesquires. Pte Saunders who had been carrying the gun had just handed it to L/Cpl Buckley when a fragment of a shell hit the gun driving it on to L/Cpl Buckley's head and killing him instantly.

Pte Saunders and the remaining 2 men of the team followed on the Dunkin Road until they struck a post on the right hand side manned by R.W.K and 140 M.G.Coy. This post would appear to be that in K.17.b.

The total casualties suffered by this Section were:

		Lieut Chanvers G.M.C.C.	Wounded & missing
22315	Sgt	Butler R	" Missing
23179	Cpl	Baxter H	" "
23204	"	Brunswick AW	" "
23210	L/Cpl	Moore A.J	" "
16012	"	Buckley F	" Killed
41900	Pte	McCulloch H	" Wounded & missing
35886	"	Derratt D	" Wounded
52623	"	Pye L	" "
52159	"	Silkin W	" "

C. P. Davis
Capt
Comdg
7.12.1917   142 Machine Gun Coy

WAR DIARY or INTELLIGENCE SUMMARY

Army Form C. 2118.

Place	Date	Hour	Summary of Events and Information	Remarks and references to Appendices
	1		Wind NE. Weather clear and bright. The Company moved to tents at VELUBART CAMP P30 & K030 HAVRINCOURT WOOD.	FRANCE 57c
	2		Wind NE. Weather clear and bright. Company obtaining any stores & equipment required. Company prepare for march out. Snow during night.	
	3		Wind NE. Weather clear and cold. Physical training during morning. The Company moved at 3 p.m. to camp in HAVRINCOURT WOOD bringing in tents by 8 p.m. remaining at VELUBART CAMP.	
	4		Wind N. Weather clear and cold. Limbers prepared for line. At 4.30 p.m. the Company (less C Section) proceeded to line to relieve the 58 L.C.T. Relief completed by 12 midnight. The dispositions of the Coys are as follows. (1) B Section H.Qrs (L20a and L19b) A Section H.Qrs in L.19.k. D Section H.Qrs in K56k. C Section at tram & VELU CANTON.	
	5		Wind N. Weather cold. Morning very quiet.	
	6		Wind NE. Weather cold. Enemy activity below normal. The transport and C Section move to transport lines at BERTINCOURT.	
	7		Wind N. Weather cold during morning. Shower set in during early evening. Snow fell during night. Enemy artillery slightly increased activity. RISECOURT and BEET TRENCH shelled with 5.9.	
	8		Wind N. Enemy activity below normal.	

Army Form C. 2118.

WAR DIARY
or
INTELLIGENCE SUMMARY.
(Erase heading not required.)

Instructions regarding War Diaries and Intelligence Summaries are contained in F. S. Regs., Part II. and the Staff Manual respectively. Title pages will be prepared in manuscript.

Place	Date	Hour	Summary of Events and Information	Remarks and references to Appendices
FLESQUIERES Right Sub Sector	Jan 9		Weather cold & windy. D Section relieved A Section during morning. To Section relieved B Section at night, B Section withdrawing to reserve in K.36.d.15.30. Enemy artillery activity slightly above normal, RIBECOURT being intermittently shelled throughout day. 1 O.R. killed and 1 O.R. wounded.	MOEUVRES 1/20,000
	10		Weather cold. Enemy artillery activity above normal. RIBECOURT and area south receiving considerable attention. Front system also shelled. During the night the dispositions of guns were altered, all guns being formed into Batteries for barrage fire. A Section moved to form A Battery at L.26.d.11.12. at 5.30pm taking over the positions from A Section of the 58 M.G.Coy. C Section moved to form B Battery at L.20.c.3.5.20. at 6.30pm. D Section moved to form C Battery at L.19.d.12.13. at 5 am on 11th. 2 O.Rs wounded.	
	11		Weather cold. Some rain during morning. Enemy artillery activity normal. At 6.18 am troops Heavy Artillery with Divisional Artillery co-operation put down barrage on troops frontage for 15 minutes; enemy retaliation slight; otherwise enemy activity normal. At night Bny HQ moved to RIBECOURT L.26.a.7.5.10. 1 O.R. killed 1 O.R. wounded. Capt. Davies proceeded on one months leave to the U.K.	

Army Form C. 2118.

WAR DIARY
or
INTELLIGENCE SUMMARY.
(Erase heading not required.)

Instructions regarding War Diaries and Intelligence Summaries are contained in F. S. Regs., Part II. and the Staff Manual respectively. Title pages will be prepared in manuscript.

Place	Date	Hour	Summary of Events and Information	Remarks and references to Appendices
FLESQUIERES Right Sub Sector	12		Weather cold. Rain during day. Hostile artillery activity below normal with exception of concentration on RIBECOURT between 11am and 1pm. The 140 Inf Bde tos M.G.Coy were relieved by the 140 Inf Bde. 8 men of A Section relieved 8 men of C Section at B Battery	MANOEUVRES 1/10000
	13		Weather fine but cold. Enemy activity normal. The 142 M.G. Coy were relieved by the 140 M.G.Coy. Relief complete by 8 p.m. On relief Sections moved independently to Billets at BERTINCOURT. Company in billets by 12 M.N. During this period of duty in the Trenches the Company suffered casualties as follows :- 2 O.R. killed, and 4 O.R. wounded. Lt. RUDDELL L. and 12 O.R. arrived from Base.	France 5/40 1/40000
BERTINCOURT	14		Weather cold but fine. Cleaning of guns and general cleaning up.	
	15		Weather cold. Much rain during day. Schools of instruction in billets and interior economy.	
	16		Weather cold. Very stormy during day. Schools of instruction in billets	
	17		Interior Economy	
	18		Interior Economy	
	19		Interior Economy and preparation for move to line. During the evening Company relieved 141 Machine Gun Coy on left Sub-Sector. Relief complete by 9.30pm Disposition :— 2guns in front system — 10 guns in forward area and barrage positions 4 guns in Reserve at K 28 a 80 95. Coy HQ at K.29 d. 16. 60.	
FLESQUIERES Left Sub Sector				MANOEUVRES 1/20000

Army Form C. 2118.

WAR DIARY
or
INTELLIGENCE SUMMARY.
(Erase heading not required.)

Instructions regarding War Diaries and Intelligence Summaries are contained in F.S. Regs., Part II. and the Staff Manual respectively. Title pages will be prepared in manuscript.

Place	Date	Hour	Summary of Events and Information	Remarks and references to Appendices
FLESQUIERES Left Sub-Sector	1918 Jan 20th		Wind SE. Weather clean and bright. Enemy artillery activity normal. Trench M at FEMY WOOD and TRIANGLE WOOD shelled with H.E. 5.9' and 8" during morning. FLESQUIERES shelled intermittently during day with L.H.V. New position for G Battery sited at K.24.d.20.70 and work on emplacements commenced at 6.30 pm. 6 gas rds fired on enemy roads and tracks in K.5a and K.6.c.	MOEUVRES K.00.00.00
	21		Wind S. Weather clear. Enemy activity below normal. K.29.a and c shelled with 5" H.E. during morning. Work on emplacements at K.24.d.20.70 continued. New Emplacements dug at L Battery L.25.b.10.75. 6 gas rds fired on mowers in K.6.c.	
	22		Enemy artillery activity slightly above normal. FLESQUIERES received the usual shelling during the day. During the morning of guns and batteries telephone mobilisation was found to be necessary at each battery for the purpose of keeping up communication between Bty HQ and batteries and also Batteries and Bde. HQ. For this purpose over 3 miles of wire has been laid during the last 3 days and batteries (L,H & G) as well connected with the various Bty Commanders where from they cover. The reserve section is in direct communication with Bty HQ and Bde HQ and also communicate with that batteries. This system has necessitated that	

Army Form C. 2118.

WAR DIARY
or
INTELLIGENCE SUMMARY.
(Erase heading not required.)

Instructions regarding War Diaries and Intelligence Summaries are contained in F. S. Regs., Part II. and the Staff Manual respectively. Title pages will be prepared in manuscript.

Place	Date	Hour	Summary of Events and Information	Remarks and references to Appendices
FLESQUIERES Left Sub Sector	1918 Jan		The present establishment of L.W. signallers should be greatly increased and arrangements were made that 6 signallers should be permanently attached to the Groups to no duty at those stations. There were reported 4 enemy Trench Mortars.	NEUVRES K.D.o.v.o
	23		Enemy activity normal. HAVRINCOURT shelled with Gas shell during morning between 3h30 and 4h00 vicinity of CEMETERY in K23d shelled with H.E. H.8 and 5.9 calibre. Enlargement of dug out at K23d 40.10 continued.	
	24		Enemy activity below normal. K22a shelled with gasshell between 1a.m. & 2 p.m. Weather clear.	
	25		Enemy artillery activity slightly above normal. FLESQUIERES vicinity usual shelling throughout day. T WOOD heavily shelled with H.E. & ? calibre. Between 4 a.m. to 7 p.m.	
	26		Weather misty. Enemy active & usual. No shelling worthy of note during day. Weather cold and misty. Enemy very quiet during day	
	27		Weather clear but cold. Enemy artillery activity normal. HAVRINCOURT	
	28		shelled with Gas shell about 6 p.m.	
	29		Weather bright. Enemy activity below normal. FLESQUIERES shelled with H.H.V. between 2 and 4 p.m. G Battery ? WIRECUTTING at K23d 60.60	

Army Form C. 2118.

WAR DIARY
or
INTELLIGENCE SUMMARY.
(Erase heading not required.)

Instructions regarding War Diaries and Intelligence Summaries are contained in F. S. Regs., Part II. and the Staff Manual respectively. Title pages will be prepared in manuscript.

Place	Date	Hour	Summary of Events and Information	Remarks and references to Appendices
FLESQUIERES Batt^n H^Q Station	1918 Jan 30		Weather cold. Enemy artillery activity below normal. FLESQUIERES shelled with	WDE IV R15S x/20000
	31		4 HV during day. Enemy activity practically nil. Weather cold but fine.	

Graham Kinn

Army Form C. 2118.

142 M.G Coy
Vol 27

WAR DIARY
or
INTELLIGENCE SUMMARY.
(Erase heading not required.)

Instructions regarding War Diaries and Intelligence Summaries are contained in F. S. Regs., Part II. and the Staff Manual respectively. Title pages will be prepared in manuscript.

142ND MACHINE GUN COMPANY

Place	Date	Hour	Summary of Events and Information	Remarks and references to Appendices
In the Field	1st-May		Brewing weather, unfitly practically nil, Companies in front line.	
	2nd		Coy. employed on usual fatigues.	
	3rd		Coy. employed on usual fatigues. During night the Company relieved by two M.G. Coys and proceeded onward and entrained at Hopt. Railway from MESCHEET.	
	4th	10 am	Arrived at BEAUCOURT by Light Railway from MESCHEET. Company marched to billets to be allotted to them.	
			During this period of duty in the trenches the personnel of the Company on the line suffered no casualties. The only casualty being one man severely (dangerously) wounded on 22.4.1918 on return journey with (B) section returning from Divl Rest. The mules of the Company suffered very considerably. During this period on the line the Company use 15 formations.	
	5th		Weather fine. Cold BATHS. Studies and troops cleaning up.	
	6th		Weather fine. Coy fatigued and carrying of tooth-brush protection & transport lines.	
	7th		C.D. transport detailed baths during morning. Resale fines Coy fatigued routine inspection Kit insp. & cleaning protection & transport lines.	
	8th		Weather fine. Coy fatigues routine inspection and work continued on cleaning horse lines & transport lines.	
	9th	9am	Weather fine. During morning general inspection were made prior to move to line, at 5pm the Company proceeded by Light Railway to MESCHEET and from there by route march to their position assigned to them by groups	

Army Form C. 2118.

WAR DIARY
or
INTELLIGENCE SUMMARY.
(Erase heading not required.)

142ND MACHINE GUN COMPANY

Place	Date	Hour	Summary of Events and Information	Remarks and references to Appendices
In the Field	10.3.18		Weather fine. Enemy artillery activity much above normal. RIBECOURT receiving attention intermittently throughout day with large calibre H.E. Smoke operation was carried out by No. 1025 + 2658 M.G. Coys in co-operation with heavy artillery as retaliation for the shelling of D. Battery during morning.	
		10.15 pm	The guns fired on 1 M.G. near the target and at 10.15 pm the heavy artillery range at the fuse for 3 minutes. Light machine guns (2 per forward company) fired a box barrage on the fds to A. & C. Batteries firing 2 guns each, each one firing 3 belts for 3 minutes.	
		11.5 pm	The operation was repeated at 11.5 pm.	
	11th		Weather misty. Enemy artillery activity normal.	
	12th		Weather misty. Enemy very quiet.	
	13th		Weather dull. Enemy activity nil.	
	14th		Weather dull. No enemy activity.	
	15th		Weather clear.	
		2.30 am	FRENY AVENUE shelled with LHV about 2.30 pm to 3.30 pm. Otherwise situation normal.	
		3.30 pm	Very quiet.	
	16th		Weather clear, bright. Enemy activity greatly above normal. RIBECOURT shelled intermittently during morning. 6000 rds fired on sunken road in L.22.a. During night.	
	17th		Weather bright. Enemy artillery and aircraft activity slightly above normal. 450 rds fired during silence. No enemy planes were with observed.	

WAR DIARY
or
INTELLIGENCE SUMMARY.

(Erase heading not required.)

Army Form C. 2118.

Instructions regarding War Diaries and Intelligence Summaries are contained in F. S. Regs., Part II. and the Staff Manual respectively. Title pages will be prepared in manuscript.

Place	Date	Hour	Summary of Events and Information	Remarks and references to Appendices
In the Field	19/17		Weather clear. Enemy artillery above normal. RIBECOURT receiving considerable attention.	
	20th		Weather dull. Enemy very quiet. About 3000 nds fired during day at aeroplanes one of which was believed to have been hit. Enemy did during night no bomb raids.	
			Enemy artillery normal. Shelling shells with gas shells. No casualties caused. 5000 nds fired on enemy roads and tracks.	
	21st		Enemy very quiet during day.	
	22nd		Weather dull. No artillery activity to report.	
	23rd		Weather dull. No artillery activity of note. During night 2 Coy's reported by No. 1 + No. 2 guns were shelled by Nos. 223 + 119 Boys R.N.D. and proceeded by Light Railway from TRESCAULT to BOIS NUAGE (?) by company in lorries to 2 a.m.	
		2 a.m.	During the period of duty in the trenches the company have only suffered one casualty. This was a slight Shrapnel wound on neck of the scout of the gun posting of A Battery on the left, although the efforts were not relieved until a 2 p.m. September. During the time only 3 and 8 were where were caused on the log.	
	24th		Weather clear. Company inspections and cleaning up.	
	25th		Weather dull. Firearms Company training.	
	26th		Weather dull. Company training.	
	27th		Men in all ranks carry Company training during the morning. Sports during afternoon.	
	28th		Death. .... during Company training.	

142ND MACHINE GUN COMPANY.

www.ingramcontent.com/pod-product-compliance
Lightning Source LLC
Chambersburg PA
CBHW081528160426
43191CB00011B/1711